Find Me

Find Me

ROSIE O' DONNELL

WARNER BOOKS

An AOL Time Warner Company

Rosie O'Donnell's profits from the sales of this book are being donated to charity.

The names and some identifying details of a few individuals in this book have been changed to protect their privacy.

Warner Books, Inc., 1271 Avenue of the Americas, New York, NY 10020

Visit our Web site at www.twbookmark.com.

 An AOL Time Warner Company

Printed in the United States of America

First Printing: April 2002
10 9 8 7 6 5 4 3 2 1

ISBN: 0-446-53007-7
LCCN: 2001098556

Book design by Giorgetta Bell McRee
Endpaper design and photos by Rosie O'Donnell

For Teach the Peach

Acknowledgments

Thanks to:

Lauren Slater for convincing me I could, then showing me how.

Binky, Kim, Jamie, and Larry for working it all out.

Anne Lamott, Nora Ephron, Dave Eggers, Fannie Flagg, Pat Conroy, and Anne Rice for writing as they do.

Kelli for putting up with me as I got it all down.

Find Me

CHAPTER 1

Come on, Bessie!" she'd say while tenderly tapping the dashboard of her rusty blue station wagon. "Come on, Bessie!" every time, without fail, urging the old car up a steep hill. I would lie in the way, way back, all alone, listening over the ever-present din of sibling arguments and wait for it. "Come on, Bessie," I'd mouth along with her. A secret ritual, a way to connect.

My dad sold Bessie sometime in the winter of 1973. I came home from school and the battered blue wagon was gone. I didn't expect an explanation, I didn't ask for one. I missed that car, full of memories, full of her. After she died, I would curl up in the way, way back, close my eyes, and search for the Mommy smell that still lingered inside. A scent that would carry me off to dreamland.

CHAPTER 2

I met Stacie for the first time in May. Her voice was meek and flat on the phone. She wasn't crying, but I heard it, the unmistakable sound of desperation. That was the first call, the single call that would change my life, and hers too, probably forever.

I work with a nonprofit adoption agency in New Jersey. I fund their operation and provide outreach services; they do the work. Finding families for kids who need them is beyond fulfilling, it is addictive. I like to help. I need to help. I help a lot, sometimes too much.

This is a true story about a girl named Stacie who called the adoption agency with a terrible problem. A lot of it won't make sense, at least logically. But sometimes sense runs deeper than logic. Nothing happens by chance. The events that follow, some dark and painful, changed me absolutely.

You have been warned.

CHAPTER 3

Once a week, after my show, I have an adoption meeting. An intake counselor gives me a rundown: who called, who returned the necessary forms, any problem cases. That's where this thing with Stacie started, but not at all where it ended. One afternoon in May I sat down with Colleen, one of our counselors. It was pretty standard fare until she opened a blue folder on her lap. "Oh, God," she said, glancing over her words, remembering. "This one is so sad." Then suddenly Colleen bit her lower lip and started to cry. At that moment I remembered why I no longer talk to birth mothers. I can't stand the pain in their voices, the tenderness in their hearts, their struggling souls. Also, I become overinvolved. To put it bluntly, I have no boundaries. Zero, nada, zippo—none. The birth mothers who call are usually in crisis—scared, confused, and needy—and I am in constant savior mode. Like it or not, I hear their voices, I see their faces, I don the tights and cape. Here I come to save the day! It's not Mother Teresa–ish, it's not a calm centered giving, a planned Zen thing; it's a compulsion. I can't help myself.

Colleen told me the details of the case: "Stacie is fourteen. She is six months pregnant. Her mother, Barb, called the hot line. She got the number off the show. Her daughter Stacie was raped, get this, by a youth minister. The guy is in jail, the kid is in shock. They were calling for information only, they don't know what they will do. The mother is kind, well spoken, concerned for her daughter, feels the baby should be placed for adoption, but will do whatever the daughter decides. God, Ro, she sounded so defeated. I didn't know what to tell her."

Right then and there, for reasons I will never completely understand, I jumped in, headfirst. I broke my own rule. I picked up the intake sheet and dialed the number, a birth mother and a birth mother's mother. A double whammy. Two helpings of hurt. The phone rang. I got an answering machine. The voice on it sounded so confident and carefree, I thought it must have been recorded months before. I heard the beep, and left a message. . . . "Hi, this is Rosie O'Donnell. . . . You called our adoption line . . . the counselor told me about your daughter. . . . If I can be of help in any way . . . questions you may have, anything, please call. We can provide financial help for counseling. . . . I know this must be horrible for you and your daughter, and I am very sorry it happened." I left my office number.

Colleen went back to work, and I finished up my adoption stuff. I tried to find a parent for a two-week-old born in a hospital prison in Utah. I checked on the status of an eight-year-old HIV-positive black girl I had been trying to place for months, with no success. Difficult things, all of them. The afternoon was bright in a Crayola kind of way, simple blue sky, yellow circle of sun outside my window. But I couldn't see any of it. My mind, for some strange reason, was wandering back to the tale Colleen had told me, the tiny child carrying a child, like one of those Russian nesting dolls, babushkas you open up to find something inside, a child within a child. A mother and a daughter. My mind would not leave what it had only heard.

A mother and a daughter.

• • •

One day, before she got sick, my mother gave me my "Are you there, God? It's me, Margaret" talk. I sat in stunned silence as she spoke of the wonders of being a woman. She showed me where her maxi pads were kept—in the top right-hand dresser drawer, under the fake Ming vase. She told me three times, because I was ten and not listening. I was in shock. I cried as she told me the details of tampons, cramping, and clots. I refused to believe my body would bleed monthly. Being a girl was horrible and gross. It was the end of the world as I knew it. First I found a lone strand of hair under my arm, and now this. I prayed it was all some sick joke mothers were forced to tell their daughters. Since she never brought it up again, I decided to forget the whole thing. Then she died.

I got my period when I was in eighth grade, during basketball practice. I went into the bathroom and saw my stained underwear, disbelieving. I was sure I had cancer, hepatitis, or diarrhea at least. I didn't know what to do or who to tell. I shoved some toilet paper into my shorts and finished the game. When I got home I took a very hot shower, scalded my skin, and wished my mother alive.

With no other choice, I snuck into my mother's room, which was now only my father's room. If anyone saw me, I was going to say I needed change for the ice-cream man. My dad had a pile of pocket coins on his dresser; I frequently helped myself to them. Once inside his room, I put a chair by the door so no one could get in. No one tried to. I saw myself in the mirror, above her dresser, a face full of want and need. I closed my eyes, so as not to see my own disappointment, and slowly pulled at the top right-hand drawer, under the fake Ming vase. My eyes opened to a blur of blue. There they were, a full box of Kotex Maxi Pads, right where she said they would be.

She must have known she was dying, that she would not be around when I needed her most. She orchestrated this comfort and care from beyond the beyond, before she left. I was fourteen the day I first needed a maxi pad. Fourteen, like Stacie.

• • •

Why this one girl, Stacie? Why did this tragedy, among all others, sit so stubbornly in my head? I'm not a naive woman. I've seen soul-smashing stuff before. Right from the start, though, Stacie stood out.

Why? Why this one kid, this particular story? I had spoken to pregnant teenage girls before. I had spoken to women who were raped. But never a child, raped, and pregnant, all at once. It was too horrible to imagine, too sickening to forget. And the tragic twist, the inedible icing on the corrupt cake—the rapist was a minister. A minister, a man society tells you is trustworthy, a man you are supposed to love and be led by. A man who should have been safe, a savior even. He was the virtuous villain. It was all too much for me. From the moment I heard the tale, I was hooked.

CHAPTER 4

I have many names. People close to me in my life call me Ro, as in "your boat gently down the stream." I was born, however, Roseann O'Donnell to Roseann O'Donnell on March 21, 1962. My stage name is Rosie, and at first I hated it.

I was working in a tiny comedy club in 1980. The comic introducing me was from Brooklyn. "Next up, RoseannAdonal," he said, all smushed together like it was one word. *Roseanna Roseannadana*—that's how it sounded to the folks in the seats. . . . They waited with expectant faces for Gilda Radner, or someone doing an impression of her. Nope, just me. When I got off stage that night, the club owner, a man who looked so much like Richard Nixon that he legally changed his name to Richard M. Dixon and opened a nightclub called The White House Inn, came over to me and said, "From now on, kid, you are Rosie O'Donnell. . . . Rosie, no

11

more Roseann. . . . It's Rosie, kid. . . . It sings . . . to the moon!" And that was that.

I don't really feel like a Rosie. Rosie is Nancy Walker selling paper towels. "Bounty, the quicker picker-upper!" Rosie is the maid on *The Jetsons*. Rosie is an elderly aunt who forces you to eat decade-old hard candies that live in the bottom of her crusty purse. No, Rosie never fit me. I feel like a Ro.

CHAPTER 5

I know stuff. Stuff I shouldn't. It scares some people. Not me. It started when I was little, before I knew what they were, these ethereal moments where I am given information from some unknown place inside me. Whatever it is tells me, and then I know.

Very Shirley MacLaine.

My brother Eddie's son was born around the same time as my daughter Chelsea. A beautiful redheaded boy, with my nana's blue eyes. He was alert and happy and not able to find a formula that would stay in his stomach. I saw him when he was two months old; I looked at him and I knew. This baby, my nephew, had cystic fibrosis. No one in my family had CF; no one in my sister-in-law's family did, either. Other than spitting up, the baby was healthy. It seems unbelievable, but I knew he had CF. I asked my brother if they had tested the baby for anything. "Like what?"

was his response. "Cystic fibrosis," I said meekly. He thought I was insane, as did everyone else. But I knew; I was sure. The baby was tested two weeks later, and he does, in fact, have cystic fibrosis. My brother thinks I should open a psychic hot line, give Dionne Warwick a run for her money. The thing is, my knowing arrives. I can't request its appearance. It happens when it happens.

I also have spingles. They are much more subtle than knowing nods. A spingle is a deep shaking shiver, the kind that climbs your spine and leaves your throat dried up. Out of the blue I'll see something, or hear something, and it will spingle up my back. It can be small things. When I was six years old, I found a bird's egg in the grass by the big tree in our front yard. It was a robin's egg, tiny, speckled blue, and perfect. I picked it up. The egg was cool and small and I thought I could feel the tiny bird beating its wings inside. I pictured the bird in its yolk world, flapping away. I took it home. I held it close in my palm, trying to let my own body heat go through the shell: *Stay warm, little bird.* At home, in the room I shared with my sister, Maureen, I put the egg under my desk lamp, in a nest of toilet paper. For four days I watched. I waited. I wanted that bird to be born, and once it was born, I figured, we'd be the best of friends. He would sit on my shoulder and repeat after me. I swabbed the egg with cotton balls and water; I sang it to sleep. It never hatched. Weeks later, overcome with curiosity, I broke it open. Inside was just a yellow crust and a scatter of feathers. Spingle.

Huge things cause spingles too. Daytwon Bennett, a five-year-old boy, starved, beaten, and found dead, tied to his crib in the Bronx. The newspaper had his photo next to the way-too-tiny item about his murder. I can still see his eyes. Certain sorts of horrors open up my skin. And now it was happening with Stacie, although back then, before the journey had really begun, I couldn't say why.

• • •

I went to therapy the day I left the message for Stacie and her mom. Just a coincidence I suppose. I told my no-nonsense shrink the whole story, a rape, a kid, a minister, and a mom. When I was finished, she said, "Ro, you have to learn to sit on your hands." She says that often.

Have you ever had a mind itch? It's like there's a tickle in your brain, or maybe a bug bite. A brain is no place for a bug to bite, but I bet if you cracked open my skull you'd see little round raised red circles. I think I have OCD or ADD or some other three-initial ditty. Whatever it is, it is exhausting. I worry. I used to spend a lot of time wondering why I worry about the things I do. Is the need to save people good or bad, compulsion or compassion? Where's the line, and how do you know when you've crossed over it? Are artists driven by creativity or insanity? It's complicated. On a good day I think I'm a relatively sane person with a few frayed wires. On a bad day I think *Just lock me up.* Maybe compassion is compulsion, creativity is insanity. If this is so, then is craziness a good thing, the source of our humanity? I ask myself these sorts of things on a daily basis. I wish I didn't. I need a pause button for my brain.

That night I put my kids to bed. I tucked in Parker, Chelsea, and then Blake, who was still an infant and in a crib. I wound up his musical mobile and watched the black-and-white shapes turn in the air. He is so sweet, my sleeping baby boy. His eyelids are very thin, and they flit back and forth. Sometimes he laughs. There is nothing, I mean nothing, as wonderful as a baby whose dreams are good. I held his little hand. I thought of the little bird egg. I thought of my own mother. Did she stand over my crib like this? She must have.

She had a big laugh, my mother, but there was never enough of her to go around. When she slept, I used to pull the loose skin on her knuckles like it was taffy, and she wouldn't wake up. Even while she slept, I wanted her attention.

I fell asleep and had an odd dream. It was raining and I was lost. In the distance were spinning lights and a huge sand castle. A black car drove by, and stopped. The window rolled down;

Angelina Jolie was behind the wheel. She wanted directions. I didn't have any. She gave me a pair of dice and told me not to worry so much. I looked up and saw a baby monkey in a very tall tree. (What the hell does that mean?)

That next morning I did my show. I walked down the hall, stopped in the nursery to see my kids, went into my office. My assistant looked up at me as I walked toward her. "Someone is on the phone, sounds like a kid, she said you gave her this number?"

It was her. I walked into my office, closed the door, and picked up the phone. "Hello?" I said.

That flat, distant, dull voice answered. "Hi, this is Stacie. My mom said I should call. . . ."

"Yes," I said, my voice catching. "Hi, Stacie, thanks for calling. . . . My name is Rosie and I will help you in any way I can."

And as I said those words, it was like a shell breaking open or a bird coming out. A connection beginning. Stacie. Stacie and Rosie and Barb, and later on—well, you wouldn't believe what joined us. You wouldn't believe what happened, what I learned about Stacie, about life, about me. I said hello and a crack came, and we all fell in, straight into looking-glass land, where nothing is what it seems, and when you finally get out it's a brand-new world, so if you looked at your palms, even your life lines would spell something totally different.

CHAPTER 6

I grew up on Rhonda Lane, the middle of five kids. We weren't rich and we weren't poor, but somewhere in that place in between, where it can be difficult to make ends meet, and you buy generic-brand everything. Our house was always a mess, laundry in piles, toys with missing pieces, and never enough Scotch tape. We had wallpaper with bubbles in it and Magic Marker–marked stairs. After my mother died, the house and just about everything else fell into total disrepair. It was always dark inside. Life itself was smeared a dull gray. It smelled of dust and stale urine. To me, it smelled of death.

My mother's mother, Nana, lived with us. Nana was so old. Her skin, if you touched it, felt like suede. I didn't touch her much. Nana's ears were going. That's what everyone said, "Oh, your nana's ears are going, you know," and when I was very young, I would think, *Going where?* A child's world is so literal. So many things don't make sense. I was a scared kid, but you'd never have known it. I'm a scared adult. I don't think it shows.

My nana lived on the top floor of our house. She'd watch TV all day, sitting two inches from the screen, with the volume blaring so loud you could hear it in every room. Whenever the phone rang she'd cry out, "Telephone . . . telephone . . ." as if we couldn't hear it ourselves. After a minute, she'd hoist herself up, wobble toward the phone, pick it up, and scream, "HEDDOOO . . . WHO'S THERE . . . HEDDOOO . . . SPEAK UP. . . ." My nana was a riot. She chainsmoked Chesterfields and often missed the ashtray altogether, leaving her place at the dinner table dotted with small black circles.

I wish I remembered more about my mother. She was a typical thick-waisted Irish woman with a round face, and dark hair, like me. My mother died in 1973; she was thirty-eight, one year younger than I am now. People loved her; she was very funny. I watched my grade school teachers flee their classrooms in order to chat with her in the hallway. Through the four-foot-square glass panel, I saw my mom perform her magic, like a silent film star. Each conversation ended with uncontrollable laughter, the kind adults try not to show in front of kids. She was good. My mom was an active lady, president of our school PTA, a member of the parish council, and a Girl

Scout troop leader. She wore little makeup—maybe a dab of pinkish lipstick. I wonder: Had she lived, would we be friends? Would our mother-daughter relationship have survived and transformed into something of substance, something I could count on?

My mother had a knickknack shelf she got at the flea market. It was an old wooden typesetter's tray she cleaned and refinished, using steel wool and sandpaper. She put red velvet on the back and a glass frame on the front, and she hung it horizontally on the wall. A rectangle full of smaller rectangles, ready to be filled with souvenirs, silver spoons, tiny vases with tinier tulips. Tchotchkes, junk. The knickknack shelf was proudly displayed in our kitchen. We weren't supposed to open it, but I did, whenever I could without getting caught. I needed to see, up close, the World's Fair tickets that were once Uncle Jim's, and the small wooden old lady that looked so much like Granny. My mom had two tiny Limoges plates and was on the lookout for a third. One Sunday we were at the flea market, browsing. My mom stopped in front of a stall full of knickknacks and spotted a plate she wanted. *It must be Limoges,* I thought, but said nothing. Then, in a voice I did not recognize, she asked meekly, "How much is this cute little plate here?" I stared at her, confused. What happened to my mother? The PTA president, the woman our local parish priest said "don't rock the boat" to twice a week. Who was this thin-voiced stranger next to me? I had to do something. I did. "Mommy," I said, "is that Limoges, like you collect?" She stepped on my foot hard enough to let me know I should shut up. I had blown her cover. The Limoges comment wasn't what she was looking for. I realized, later, that she had been acting, my mom, like a little unknowing house-wife in an effort to get a better deal. The man behind the counter smiled and told her the price was firm. We walked away empty-handed. Before we got to the next booth she told me, "Never say *Limoges* at a flea market." Advice I follow to this day.

My mother. No one speaks of my mother. Not then, not now. I knew she was dying. No one told me she was, but I knew. In my house you had to go with your gut. With no one around to answer the questions, I made up my own. I made a judgment, I deduced, I calculated, I became an authority on nearly nothing and almost everything. I taught myself to juggle, to spin a ball on one finger, to balance a chair in the palm of my hand. Simple skills that gave me a feeling of safety, or superiority. I can do many amazing card tricks, and although I know the magician's code says you should not reveal the secrets, I do so, willingly, to anyone who asks. I know the peace found in knowing the truth, the sham, the unspoken.

My mother was dying, I was pretty sure. My dad told me she had hepatitis. I looked it up in the school dictionary. Hepatitis was a disease transmitted through dirty needles. I vowed never to use the sewing machine.

She was in the hospital again, the last time I saw her; she didn't look so good. Our house had become creepy quiet in her absence. You could almost hear the cellos and violas, dark ominous chords. Something bad was happening, I felt it. It was early March 1973; the day was gray, spring had not sprung. My dad was in the playroom, staring out the window, smoking. I was in the hallway, by the closet, full of button-filled mayonnaise jars and mismatched rubber boots.

"Is Mommy going to die?" I asked him. He didn't move, my father. I was not sure he had heard me. I thought about asking again, but did not. I waited. Nothing. Finally, after a few moments, he said faintly and without much conviction, "I hope not." He did not turn to me and look into my eyes reassuringly. It was obvious the conversation was over.

He never learned to swim, my dad. He saw the tide was rising. He tried his best to tread water, keeping his head barely above the surface, counting—I am sure—the bobbing heads of his children in the surf. By St. Patrick's Day we would all be fully submerged.

She died. She remains a mystery to me.

I know two things she loved, show tunes and Streisand. My mother adored Barbra, and so did I. While other kindergartners were bringing in kaleidoscopes and turtles for show-and-tell, I was belting "Don't Rain on My Parade" with gusto, off-key, complete with dance moves. I would memorize every Streisand record, and when my mother was cooking dinner, I would put on a show in the kitchen. "Second Hand Rose" and "Marty the Martian." She would laugh, my mom. I loved it.

I told her once, on the way down the church steps, the morning of my first communion, that when I grew up I was going to become a nun. "No you're not, the pay is horrible."

When I was sure she was dying, but not sure what of, I decided I would have to become famous. My kid logic was that if Barbra Streisand's mom was sick, Barbra would go on the Johnny Carson show and ask everyone who loved her to send in a dollar. Everyone would. They would get a thousand dollars and be able to get medicine for her mom. Fame, I thought, at ten, could fix everything, even disease.

After she died, I'd sneak into New York City with money stolen from my dad's wallet. I'd hop the Long Island Railroad and go see a Broadway show. The ushers got to know me and would let me in at intermission; I saw the second act of nearly every show from 1975 to 1980. I would become an actress, I was sure. At thirteen, I would

24

sit on the sink in the upstairs bathroom and pop my pimples, while having a conversation with Johnny Carson about the fact that when I was a kid, I used to sit on the sink in the upstairs bathroom and pretend to be talking to him. That's some creative visualization. I understand now that I thought fame and the fantasyland of the movies would save me. In fact I was certain it would protect me from scary dreams and dead mothers and a nana whose ears were going, going, gone.

My mother died on March 17, 1973. She did not have hepatitis as I'd been told. She had breast cancer.

I've since learned a lot about breast cancer. I have written a book about it. I have had a few suspicious-looking cysts removed from my breasts. So far I am healthy, but I worry that I too will get this disease. In researching my breast cancer book, I got to see slides of healthy and cancerous breast tissue. I got to see actual lumps from lumpectomies. In doctors' offices I have peered beneath microscopes at other women's illnesses, and in them I have seen the original woman, who is dead now, but still lives in me.

I have also seen healthy breast tissue. Maybe because my mother died of breast cancer, or maybe because every female has a fear of this disease, there are few things quite as lovely to me as healthy breast tissue seen under a microscope.

The cells are abundant and exuberant, like hydrangeas. They are pink-purple in color.

Near the end of her life, my mother lived on the living room couch. I would do my homework in that room, on the floor, just to be near her. She taught me, in those final weeks, how to use a dictionary. Now, when I am stuck for a spelling, I grab the big book, ignoring the spell-check feature on my swanky top-of-the-line computer, and remembering her lesson in alphabetical order. *ABCD. XYZ.* The end of the line.

I remember her near the very end, so thin, wasting away before my eyes. Her friend, our neighbor Mrs. Nordin, would come over and sit with her. One day they tried Nair on my mom's legs. Mrs. Nordin had it all set up: washcloths, soapy water, an old green towel, tubs of Nair. I watched from the top of the staircase, pure terror in my face. My mother looked up, saw me there, and called for me to come down. I did. There was an awkward silence. Never speak the truth, that's the rule. See her die before your eyes, but say nothing. She spoke: "Little Roseann, am I Twiggy or am I Twiggy?" Then my mother laughed and so did Mrs. Nordin, and so did I. I didn't know who Twiggy was, but I knew I should laugh. I wanted to laugh. I wanted to cry.

My mother went back to the hospital sometime after Christmas. Huntington Hospital did not allow child visitors. My father had to sneak us in, one at a time, through the basement, up the emergency elevator in the back. My last visit there, the elevator stopped on the main floor, the doors opened, noise and chaos, a woman on a stretcher, blood everywhere, doctors and nurses trying to keep her alive, as my dad and I pressed our spines into the wood paneling. A doctor screamed, "What the hell is the kid doing in here?" I squeezed my father's hand, saying nothing, wishing I would wake up from the bad dream that had become my life. We made it to her room. No one said it, but this was good-bye. Her face was so pale I couldn't tell where it ended and the pillow she lay on began. She was weak and sleeping almost all the time at this point. When I walked in she opened her eyes. Have you ever seen eyes just before they enter death? They do not get dimmer, they get brighter. They shine with all the lights and flickers a person has ever seen in her whole history. They shine with rage and fear and maybe even hope. My mother's eyes were Irish blue. She opened them, and we stared straight at each other, so hard you could almost hear the click in space where our gazes met, Mom.

What was in that look? Was there love there? I think so. Were there wishes there? Most definitely yes. Wishes for me, that I might be happy one day, that we could have had more time, that I could have been easier for her, less bluster and bravado, which, as a child, were my tendencies. The important thing here, that click in space.

I was at my best friend Jackie's house playing "Mystery Date" when the phone rang. Mrs. Ellard answered it and went into the living room, fully extending the curly cord. She called to me, from behind the wall where I could not see her face, and told me to go home. She had never told me to go home before. I didn't ask why.

There were many strange cars in my driveway. I walked into the house and sat with my brothers and sister at the kitchen table. Adults I did not know stood in the dining room, staring at the five of us as if we were on stage and they were the audience. My father walked over to the table. Some adults started crying then, so some of us started crying too. My father stood in front of us for forever, it seemed, and finally, quietly, as if he had been cued, he said, "Your mother has passed away."

I both knew and did not know what he meant. *Passed away* was all we got. The rest is a blur. Passed away. I did not cry, not then. I went outside and played hockey, for hours, till it got too dark. I did put down my stick, for just a moment, as the last bit of sun was slipping away, and looked up toward the sky. I expected a sign, a signal, something. There was nothing but darkness. Passed away.

I did not go to my mother's funeral. I went to her wake. It was quite a scene. Adults screamed and cried as I made my way toward the coffin, knowing and not. I saw my stiff sleeping mommy and realized, right then, that she wasn't going to wake up. Then I cried, I cried very hard. I remember Maureen and I were holding hands, standing scared, not knowing what to do. Then we were picked up and ushered into the blue station wagon. Someone decided we weren't going to the funeral. We didn't.

On the day I got my driver's license, I went to visit my mother's grave for the first time. It is very odd reading a headstone with your own name on it. My name, her name too. Knowing her body was right there, beneath the name we share, beautifully etched in granite. I'd brought her flowers, forget-me-nots and hydrangeas, like clusters of healthy cells. All for you, Mom. My mother, the place of many wishes and longings. And to that woman, I feel I never really got to say a full good-bye. Sometimes I think that may be why I'm still saying good-bye, today. It's like I'm somehow stuck. Mom, Mom. You could just call out forever.

CHAPTER 7

I didn't think my upcoming summer would be about Stacie. I thought it would be what it always was, three full months of quiet bliss in the most beautiful place in the world. Miami is perfection to me. The first time I ever set foot in the city, I knew I was home. I love the humidity, the Hispanic flair, the glorious beaches. One day I will live there full time, healthy, tan-skinned, raising my kids in the constant summer sun.

My first trip to Florida, many years ago, was to visit Madonna in her spacious bayside mansion. This was the summer before *A League of Their Own* opened. I was amazed at the beauty of the place, the serenity I felt surrounding me. I set my sights on getting a home like the one I was in. I'd drive around and look at the Spanish villas, with their private patios and tropical, Hawaiian Punch–colored flowers, and dream.

You gotta dream it to live it—Dr. Phil says that,

on *Oprah*, all the time. I like Dr. Phil, but sometimes I wanna smack him. He once told an obese woman that she was fat because she chose to be. "Yeah" I screamed at the TV, "and you're bald 'cause you *choose* to be!" If only life were as simple as one of his sayings. It ain't. *Dream it to live it!* is in my mind, as close as you are gonna come to a one-sentence salvation. It has been true for me, 100 percent. I dreamed the life I am now living, here in Miami, in my house on the water, Spanish style with a coral-colored roof and a huge banyan tree in the front yard. Sometimes, sitting on the dock, I imagine my mother walking toward me, and wonder what she would think.

•   •   •

She lives, in my dreams. She is in California, with long black hair, like Rita Coolidge; she is a hippie. She sells flowers for a living. She doesn't need much. She hated having five kids before she was forty, so she left. She up and left, simple as that. My father finally broke down and told me the truth, no she was not dead, not at all. He was guilt-ridden, it was time for him to tell me, so he did. It was a huge cover-up; the funeral, a fake. She agreed to lie in the casket during the wake so we would believe she was gone, passed away, but she wasn't really. She held her breath as we walked up to view her body. Everyone

32

started yelling, crying, to distract us, to pull us away, so my mom could breathe again. When we left the funeral parlor, she got up and hitched her way west. Well, I had always suspected as much, I wasn't surprised. I left my father, mid-sentence, and began my search. I would find her, no matter how long it took. I wound up in front of an old beachfront bungalow in Venice, California. The place was run-down and weathered. I saw her through the dirty front window. She looked different but felt the same. It was her, my mom, I was sure. I opened the rental car door, and then I woke up. When I did, in the middle of my first alive/dead mother dream, I didn't know where I was or what was real. First confusion, then brief hope, finally again eternal sadness.

• • •

Stacie's voice over the phone was always very meek, kidlike and familiar. Our first conversation that day at the office was brief. I don't even really remember very much of it. She said she could feel the baby moving inside her and it felt like tickles, but not good tickles. Then there was a long pause. Then she told me she got the new 'NSYNC cassette. My God, I thought, she's a fourteen-year-old kid, in love with Justin and Joey, and she's about to have a baby. It seemed terrible to me. As a general rule, mothers should not be teenyboppers.

I told her I had met the 'NSYNC boys, and she came to life.

— No way?
— Way.
— Where?
— Burger King at the mall . . . duh. . . . My show, of course.
— Grown-ups don't say duh!
— Do too . . . duh.
— You're weird.
— Duh!
— Is Justin the best looking?
— Depends on your type.
— Not for me, like in real life.
— Well, it wasn't real life, it was TV.
— That's real life.
— No, in fact, it isn't.
— Did they smell?
— Smell? As in B.O.?
— No, like shampoo or guy perfume or cookies?
— I didn't notice really. I think they smelled average.
— They don't smell average. Every magazine says they each have a smell. Lance smells like cotton candy, and Joey like pizza and JC like aftershave and Justin like gummy bears and Chris like crayons. That's what every magazine says.

— Well, when they were on my show, they didn't smell like anything.

— Yeah. You wanna talk to my mom?

— Sure.

So, that was that. Our conversation had gone well, her mother seemed happy that the kid was happy, and that made me happy. Before I hung up, I gave Barb my home phone numbers in both New York and in Miami. She did not ask for the numbers, I offered, gave them freely, and told her if they needed to talk they could call, anytime.

A few days went by, no word from them. I thought of Stacie quite a bit. I said hello to her on the air, guessing she was in her room alone, watching, smiling, feeling for a moment special, cared for, full of hope. I knew Stacie was tiny— "ninety-six pounds soaking wet," according to her mother. I imagined she had dirty blond stringy hair and laser-blue eyes. I thought of her little girl body swelling with this unwanted baby. I thought of the trusted youth minister, safe and handsome, ripping the mask from his face, revealing the monster beneath, as this terrified girl was attacked. It made me nauseous, yet I couldn't shake it from my brain.

We had only a few weeks left of shows before I went to Miami, and after each one, I asked my assistant Merrie if anyone had called for me. Merrie gave me the look. She has a daily phone sheet a foot long. Who, she wanted to know, was anyone? I told her the sketchy truth, a kid, raped, pregnant, the adoption hot line, blah blah. Merrie nodded; she knows me too well. "Stacie and Barb . . . I will put them on "FIND YOU." FIND YOU is my unofficial VIP list. When anyone on it calls, they find me.

So the cat was out of the bag. Merrie knew I had once again stepped in where I should not have. Stacie was not the first person I've ever tried to help, to save. I am always in savior mode. On the lookout for anyone in trouble. In the summer of 1997 I was Jet Skiing in Miami on a beautiful hot day. Two friends were with me, out for their first run on the WaveRunners. There is a huge passageway in Miami's South Beach called Government Cut. It is where the cruise ships and tanker ships come through to port to be unloaded and reloaded before going back out to sea. There is a rock jetty, about a mile long, that stretches from the shore into the sea. Fishermen climb out there to fish; sometimes adventurous kids try to see how far they can get, too. So I was loving the sun, tooling around, and I saw three teenage girls on the far end of the jetty. They had walked out when the tide was rising, and now they were stranded, with no way back. They were not dressed for swimming, and even if they had been, it was more than a mile back to shore. I cruised up to them and saw they were crying. They must have been thirteen, maybe fourteen at the most. They told me in Spanish that they did not know how to swim. Perfect! Rosie to the rescue. I made my way through the rocks, as close to them as I could come without losing the WaveRunner. I took them, one at a time, back to shore. Each time I went back into the rocks to get another girl, I cut my leg or hand, but I didn't notice, 'cause I was focused. My friends Mimi and Carolyn were watching from a safe distance; the rocks were dangerous, and the water crashing into them, hard to ride. So I am about to drop the last girl off at the beach, she is still crying, thanking me. She asks me to come to her church so we could thank God together, the four of us. I told her thanks but no, I was going back to New York that night. She kissed me on the cheek, squeezed my hand, and said "I love the Tom Cruise too!" I drove back to my friends, who were both alarmed because I was a bloody mess, scratches and scrapes everywhere, from being thrown against the rocks time and again. I loved it; it didn't hurt at all. Pure adrenaline. I am a hero. Right? Well, no.

Sometimes my savior complex gets out of hand. In October I cursed out the mother of a terminally ill kid. I am not proud of it, but it is true. A distraught mother wrote me a letter: Her eight-year-old son was quite sick. He watched the show daily, was too weak to attend a taping, but she wanted me to know how much joy I had brought him. The letter had the right balance of tragedy and need, and they wanted nothing. Don't ask me for anything. Show me your wounds, and wait for me to come save you. I will. Ask, and I will turn away, wondering where you got the nerve. That's me, "the queen of nice." Merrie called the family, told them I would be in their city in a few weeks, said I would love to meet them. They showed up, the boy was adorable, his brothers were with him. I gave them show stuff, took photos, and went on to my meeting. I also left the mom my office number, on the off chance that if her son was well enough to travel, she should call for tickets to the show. She thanked me, but doubted he would ever be healthy enough to make the trip. Well, the boy got better, because his family came to the show not once, not twice, but three times. We do not always have room for all the Make-A-Wish kids who want to come to the show. We have only 178 seats. Terminally ill kids often end up waiting for months, or watching from the green room. Now, maybe the boy's mother was unaware of this. Maybe she didn't know there were other sick kids waiting for seats. Maybe she thought her son deserved more, had not had enough. I will never know. She kept calling, asking for more tickets. Merrie told her, at my request, that since they had been there three times, no more tickets were available. There were other children we needed to accommodate. The mom was annoyed and decided to write me a letter. Bad news is, I actually read it. It arrived on a particularly bad day. The mom said I was hurting her son by not allowing him to come again. It was his birthday soon, and he wanted to see the show as a birthday gift. Okay, now my heart starts pounding, I am engulfed in rage.

She was happy to hear from me. I went ballistic.

"Are you insane? Do you think your son is the only sick kid in the world? You have been here three times already. *Enough!* What the hell are you teaching him anyway? Your request is totally out of line and inappropriate!"

So was my rage at her, but I wasn't too concerned with me at that moment. I had done my part, I was expecting her to do hers. Didn't she get the script?

The Celebrity and the Sick Kid

Celeb	-	Hi, what's your name?
Kid	-	(give name)
Celeb	-	Nice to meet you. How old are you?
Kid	-	(give age)
Celeb	-	Here's some stuff I got for you. (give stuff)
Kid	-	Thanks, I feel better already.
Celeb	-	I am glad you do.
Kid	-	Can I take a picture with you?
Celeb	-	Sure. (pose for picture)

The end.

My giving is impulsive, driven by a demon who also happens to have a huge heart. The contradiction exhausts and embarrasses me.

CHAPTER 8

She was in seventh grade, I was in eighth. She had straight blond hair with bangs and very big boobs. That's what Brett Sumner called them on *Match Game 75*. Before Brett, no one called them anything.

She was a beautiful girl, with smoky sky-blue eyes.

There was mystery surrounding the whole escapade; details were sketchy. The football field, some popular tough boys, the brothers from around the block. Beer, a keg, maybe some vodka. Something happened. Something bad happened. All the boys and just one girl, drunk, doing things to the boys, all the boys, while the others watched.

It was Monday, and this had happened on the weekend. The boys were in school, the girl was not. There was a lot of talking, hushed whispers and closed doors. Rumors were flying. All the boys were brought to the principal's office, with their parents. Something was going down, something big.

There was no announcement, school assembly, letter to take home. The boys were gone, expelled for only one day. By Wednesday they were back in class, laughing, smiling, not at all what I expected. I looked for regret in their smirking eyes, some hint of grief or pain. There was none to be found. These boys were proud, nearly strutting. I watched them from the distance, transforming right before my eyes, from shy boys of my youth to predatory midnight men. Men of danger. Men to fear.

The blond girl was on the kickline; I remember seeing her in the uniform, on game day. All blue and white and girly-girl. In Sawmill Junior High School she cheered for the boys' teams, while I captained the girls'. I had never spoken to her.

She came back to school two weeks later. I saw her in the hall, clutching her textbooks to her chest, trying to cover up, to disappear. She walked slowly as if underwater or covered in syrupy sludge. Shame seeped out of her; I felt its pulse. I tried to catch her eye in the hallway, to nod at her, to wordlessly let her know she was not alone. But she looked down as she made her way to and from class, avoiding everyone, including me.

I was at basketball practice after school. I went

into the hallway to get a drink from the water fountain. I heard them before I saw them, the boys from the football field. They were on top of the stairwell, hidden from my view, taunting the blond girl as she made her way toward the gym. Toward me. She and I were the only ones in the hall. Twenty feet from each other, on a collision course. She was, as always, looking down as the boys kept it coming, thick and constant, the list of her "sins." She was a whore, slut, cunt, dick smoker, on and on, as she stepped closer and closer to me. My heart was pounding. I felt a silent screaming chaos, indescribable rage. I looked at the gym door; I could escape! The boys had not seen me, the girl might have, I was not sure. Then, as if the clock was ticking down on a game show, the mental music blaring, I stepped out from my hiding space. I looked up at the boys I feared and took a deep breath. I told them to shut up. That they were the ones charged with statutory rape, not her. I spit my words at them, pointedly. I said it and stood there stunned. What had I just done? I waited for their response.

There was none.

They said nothing. These big tough boys, the scary "almost men," turned in to the upstairs hallway and disappeared, leaving just me and the blond girl. She kept walking during the whole scene, her pace steady, head down, ignoring the circus that had become her life. She stopped next to me, took her left hand from the books covering her chest, and placed it on my left forearm. She said nothing. She didn't look at me. She held my arm there for a few minutes, in silence. Then let go and walked past me, out the door, into the street. She never said a word.

Spingle.

I knew, right then, my future would be better than my past. Some central core, I, emerged and demanded to be seen.

CHAPTER 9

From the very beginning, I knew Stacie would be different. She pulled at me, the phantom fourteen-year-old always on my mind. I read up on 'NSYNC in preparation for our next phone conversation. I waited, but she never called. I thought she would. She didn't. I was worried. I started to pick at my skin, to pull at the loose flesh around my knuckles, trying to wake myself up.

Finally, two weeks later, the phone rang. I have caller ID and I saw a strange area code come up, but no name. Why no name? I have advanced phone features that give me name plus phone number on my caller ID, but in this instance the name was blocked, or nonexistent. I should have thought something right then and there, but I didn't.

It was late at night. It was maybe eleven-thirty, after the evening news, my kids, every one of them asleep. Now, to be fair, Stacie lived in a different time zone; it was three hours earlier where she was.

"Hi," she said. "Rosie? It's Stacie. I'm really really sorry to call you. I . . ."

"Hey, Stace, how are you, I was worried about you."

There was a long pause.

"I don't want no baby," she said.

My God, to hear her say it, this baby, who didn't want the baby she was about to have. "I know, honey, that's why your mom called me," I said. "Because I have an adoption agency and we can find the baby a good home."

"But I don't want to *have* the baby," she said. "You know."

"You mean, give birth?"

"Yeah."

"Okay—well," I said, "there are good doctors with good medicine, you don't have to feel any pain."

Again, a long pause. I waited for her reply. I was anticipating the next series of questions, ready for whatever she threw at me.

"Hey," she said, "do you drive a limo?"

"No," I said. "I drive a minivan."

"I thought all stars drove limos."

"Not this star," I said, smiling.

"You don't sound like you," she said.

"What do you mean?"

"I mean, you sound different than on TV."

46

I had heard this before, from disbelieving QVC telephone operators and sick kids in ICU. It always gives me the creeps, like I am some huge fake, some scary clone of myself. Am I? I don't sound like me.

"Well, it's me, Rosie," I said, but, somehow, it wasn't convincing.

"How can I really know that?" Stacie said, her voice very soft, superserious, like she was asking a deep philosophical question, which, in a way, I guess she was.

I paused there for a minute. How could she know? How could I prove it? I couldn't.

"I guess," I said, "I guess, Stace, you just gotta believe."

"When I was a kid," Stacie said, and this phrase cracked my heart in half, like she wasn't a kid anymore, "when I was a kid I used to be afraid another girl who looked just like me would come and take my place and how would my mother know, if this girl looked exactly like me? So I told my mother she could always be sure it was me by a special sign."

"And what was the sign?"

"If I held two fingers in the air, then we'd know, for sure, it was me and not an alien."

"Oh yeah? Did it work?" I asked.

"So far," said Stacie.

• • •

I fell asleep. I dreamed of circus clowns and spaceships and, once again, Angelina Jolie. I dream of her a lot, more than the average person, I suspect. I asked my shrink, "Why do I keep dreaming of Angelina Jolie?" She said, "My guess would be, Angelina Jolie." Then she charged me three hundred dollars. Whatever.

• • •

At 3 A.M. the phone rang again. I heard my answering machine click on and then the voice, whispering, "Rosie, Rosie, you there, I gotta talk," and she was crying, and I bolted out of bed like it was one of my own kids, grabbed the phone. "Stacie, I'm here. What is it? Did something happen?"

I was groggy from sleep. "God," Stacie said, "you sound like a frog."

"You wake me up to tell me this?" I said.

"I'm sad," she said. "I can't sleep. I'm really, really sorry to call, I'm going to hang up—"

"Don't hang up!" I said with an urgency I did not understand.

We were quiet then. But between us the line was so clear, I could almost hear all the small sounds of Stacie's night, wind in the trees in their junk-filled front yard, a rusty swing set that no longer held swings.

"My best friend isn't talking to me anymore," Stacie said.

48

"Why's that?"

"Oh, I don't know," Stacie said. "We had this fight. What kind of kid were you?"

That question caught me off guard. I didn't have time to prepare an answer. I didn't have a script, a punch line, crib notes, nothing. That's how it would be with Stacie, the whole time. I found myself saying things to her, deep in the middle of the night, that I wouldn't necessarily say to anyone else; sometimes things I hadn't quite admitted to myself.

"Oh," I said, "I was a good athlete and kinda popular and all, but I had a crappy childhood. I was scared a lot. We didn't have a lot of money, and my mom had died. . . ."

"You sound really sad," said Stacie. "Don't be sad."

• • •

I am a busy woman. I have a career that's more like four careers. If my life were a car, it would be in fifth gear. Part of this is out of fear, I think. I despise neutral, first makes me anxious, second bores me; I like speed, or should I say, I need it. What am I avoiding?

I have no concept of time. I am always late. Every Sunday night at eight-fifty Kelli, my always-early partner, yells from the den, "Five minutes till S. J. P." Meaning *Sex and the City*, one of my favorite shows, is about to start. I yell over my shoulder, "Gimme a minute," and I do think it will be only a minute . . . but a minute becomes an hour, maybe two. I get lost in whatever I am doing. And I end up seeing *maybe* the last five minutes, Sarah's Doogie Howser–esqe ending monologue. Before I watch *Six Feet Under*, I call Carolyn, my best friend, Harvard graduate and HBO high-muck-a-muck, and ask her to send me the episode I once again missed.

I am very busy. Decoupage can take over my life. First there are the images to tear out of magazines, then edges to be shaped. Then wrapping paper to use as a base. Then the gluing and drying and coat after coat of varnish. I have been known to spend six hours on one picture frame. I bought myself a new Mac computer so I can make my own music videos. I have hundreds of digital home movies of my kids, set to music, with fade-ins and pastels. Each three-minute movie takes ten hours to make. I spend hours with my scrapbooks, photo albums. I have amazing pictures of my kids, and I can get very obsessive, arranging them to perfection. I tell myself I'm doing what my parents never did for me, giving my children a visual archive. At deeper moments of honesty, though, I see, sometimes photos are easier than actual people.

• • •

The phone calls with Stacie became a regular thing. This was still May, just before the summer of show reruns was going to begin. She'd call me late at night and then, in the morning, I'd call her mother Barb just to let her know what was up. I didn't tell Barb all the details of what we talked about, just that we were talking. Barb said her husband, Doug, was very distressed about Stacie. I offered to speak to him, like I was some kind of expert, like I would have known what to say. I heard a rustling in the background, the sound of kids. "No, he is kinda grumpy and shy and, well, I doubt he would get on the phone." I told her to let him know he could call if he wanted.

I had this nightlife with Stacie, this entangled codependent stuff, and I really didn't tell very many people about it. No one would understand; no one ever does. I act irrationally, I defy the odds, I engage when others would run. I look for trouble, I seek chaos, it is a burden. Who would I tell?

Sometimes, talking to Stacie, I'd hear these odd little shifts in her voice, personality, temper. She sounded mostly shy and kidlike, but at times she was so far away I could not reach her. I knew Stacie had many sides, shifts, and splits in her, as I had in me.

At night I was a kid talking to a kid, a mother talking to a daughter, a victim with a victim. But then the day would come, hard, glossy New York days, and I'd be up and at 'em by 7 A.M. Strange how, after being up half the night with Stacie, I didn't feel that tired during the day. I don't eat breakfast. I dislike the feel of food in the morning. Parker goes to school; Chelsea and Blake come with me to the studio, where they have a tiny schoolroom I love. My office is painted a cheery yellow, with shabby-chic couches done in soft denim and striped pillows. My assistant Merrie has curly long hair she wears pulled back with a butterfly barrette. There are coolers stocked with Perriers, Slim-Fast shakes, and Snickers bars. In my studio, it feels like nothing can go wrong.

So during the nights there was Stacie and me, and during the days there was show biz and me. Two separate mes. I'd get to my studio early in the morning. I'd review the notes. I'd go to my dressing room, sit through an hour of hair and makeup, both of which I loathe. I get dressed, I am ready, I go through the curtain and do it. I don't get nervous anymore. Truth is, sometimes, now, my show even bores me. The real people never bore me—the staff, the guests—but all the machinery of fame and the media, it gets old.

When I decided to do a talk show, I signed on for a four-year deal. In success, the money became obscene, and the studio assumed I would re-sign, as the cash was impossible to refuse. I did re-sign, but only for two years. I knew at the end of my run on the show, my oldest son would be entering second grade. This would be the perfect time to go, in my mind. I find fame quite odd, hard to deal with, nearly toxic, and I am an adult. I cannot imagine what it feels like to a child.

During his first week of kindergarten, Parker had his first real playdate. I watched his blond head as he climbed up the stairs of our seven-story town house, trailed by two classmates. They were headed to his bedroom full of Batman, or the toy room of blocks and LEGO. He was chatting, over his shoulder, casual and confident. I was on the computer, not paying much attention, when I heard the word *bodyguard*.

"I have a bodyguard and he protects me and I am going to Disney World on a private jet." I sat in stunned silence, dumbfounded. Surely I misheard. A moment later they came running back down the stairs. I called my five-year-old boy over. I tried to remain calm. "Park, did you just say you have a bodyguard and are going to Disney on a private jet?" And with a face that betrayed no guilt, shame, or awkwardness, he said yes. Then he ran down the stairs to join his friends.

The truth is, we do have a bodyguard, and we were going to Disney on a private jet, but I assumed my children would feel the same way I do about all that. It is an insanely embarrassing position to be in, it should be ignored and never discussed, it is almost shameful. At least to me. I grew up wanting; my kids have not.

I felt inferior to the kids from "Dix Hills." I have gone from Rhonda Lane, through Dix Hills, and beyond. My kids are rich, and spoiled, and they have had no suffering to balance out the gross excess that has become my life, that has always been theirs. The worst fate is to become what you loathe. Even worse, to have your kids become the ones who used to loathe you.

When I put him to bed that night, I tried to explain it to him, but the words weren't coming as I wished they would. I fumbled around subjects; how having stuff means nothing, why we have security for our family, that the plane we fly in is not ours—it belongs to the company I work for—how talking about bodyguards and cutting the line at Disney World is not cool. He could tell, from my tone, that he had done something wrong, but he wasn't sure what it was. He started to cry, and told me he gets confused. It broke my heart. It *is* confusing. I held him and rocked him to sleep.

I thank God he is only five. I remember little, if anything, from when I was five. I hope for him that there is still time for something resembling a "normal" life.

• • •

A few months into my relationship with Stacie, Jim, a studio executive, came into my dressing room, postshow. I was wiping down my face with a moist towel. My favorite part of makeup is taking it off. I love the feel of the cool air hitting your honest-to-God skin, and the beige gunk lifting right off your pores so you tingle.

Jim's a man I respect, with a tad of a Republican bent, but a vastly liberal and beautiful wife. He wears shiny shoes. "Rosie," he said, "your ratings are better than ever. We would like to renew the contract sooner rather than later."

I wasn't expecting that. I just looked at him.

He touched his nose. "You are renewing, aren't you?"

"Well, Jim, actually I am thinking no."

"Oh come on, Rosie," he said, "your show is the best thing going on daytime TV."

I laughed. "That's nice of you to say, but there may be other things, other interests . . ."

I didn't finish my sentence. I was thinking about the conversation I'd had the night before with Stacie. She had said, in her typical meek but extremely direct way, "So what's fame like for you?" I didn't think; I just spoke the truth I knew but hadn't been willing to utter. I said, "Stacie, I used to think fame would fix everything. That I would get there, and it all would be better, everything that had happened would stop hurting, and all the new things wouldn't hurt at all. Like paradise or heaven. I was wrong." After I'd said those words, I couldn't fall back asleep. I'd literally been up all night, trying to figure out what I meant. The hair, the makeup, the glitz, the glamour, it is pretend, empty. It is not as it seems.

"Look," said Jim. "You can pursue other interests, along with your show. You grow with your show, Rosie," he told me. "You and your show are one. You are a brand."

Yeah, me and Kleenex. Besides, if we were one, than why did I feel like two—a woman on the air, funny, coveting absurdity, and a woman off the air with holes in her?

"I don't know, Jim," I said.

"Rosie," he said, "of course you'll sign. We'll get you whatever you need. You'll sign, it is millions of dollars, no one walks away from that," he said with finality as he walked out of my dressing room. I wiped the fakeness from my face.

• • •

That afternoon I had my six-month mammogram. I've adjusted to the mammograms. My breasts are full of knots and lumps. I sit in the room with all the other waiting women and for that half hour I am Every Woman, Any Woman; I feel united with all the pale and anxious faces.

Getting a mammogram hurts some women, but not me. I am so happy to have one, any discomfort is irrelevant. The technician called me in. She put my breast between the metal plates, clamped down. "Are you okay?" she asked. "Fine and dandy," I replied. The machine whirred and clicked. I saw the slides only minutes later. Up there on the light box were images of my breasts, microcalcifications like specks of salt. "No changes," the doctor said. "You are okay. Come back in December."

December. By then Stacie would have had her baby. The funny thing was, I was actually counting the days of her pregnancy like it was my own. I've never been pregnant and I never will be. I am getting old, and had both fallopian tubes removed because of odd-looking cysts that the doctors wanted out. Sometimes this feels like a loss to me—that I am a woman and yet will never know what it feels like to have a baby. I obsess about giving birth, not because I think I could love that child any more than I do my own. My love for my children is absolute, unquestioning. It's not the love I'm wondering about; it's the brute body, what it can do and how I will never really know its possibilities.

When I got home the phone was ringing. "Rosie, it's Barb." She sounded stressed.

"Is everything okay?" I said. "Is Stacie okay?"

"I don't know," Barb said. She sounded close to tears. "As she gets bigger, showing more, kids are taunting her. I think we need to get her out of Oregon. She went to the movie theater this afternoon and the kids were just awful. Now she's in her room and won't speak."

I was making it up as I went along, trying so

hard to find an answer. "Do you think," I said, "maybe she could come to New Jersey, until she gives birth? Maybe I could find her a place, someone to stay with her, someone qualified."

"Rosie, we don't mean to impose on you like this—"

"Hey, it is not a problem," I said. I was lying, it was a problem, a huge problem.

"Really?" said Barb.

"I swear, let me work on it," I answered.

I hung up with Barb, called my lawyer. Because Stacie was a pregnant minor, there were legal issues about having her cross state lines. "Are you insane?" my lawyer shouted. "You want to rent an apartment for a fourteen-year-old girl, have someone baby-sit her till she pops, and you've *never even met her*? As your lawyer, Rosie, I need to tell you this is a bad idea."

"Yeah, and it is a bad idea to have an adoption agency to begin with," I said, and hung up on him.

He called me right back. He knows me.

"*A bad idea*," he shouted as soon as I picked up. "She's probably hoodwinking you. Have you even seen a sonogram? How do you know she's really pregnant? She probably wants your *money!* It's about money! You're an easy mark, O'Donnell—all I'd have to do is get a boo-boo on my thumb and you'd set up a trust fund for me."

"For you, never!" I said, heavy on the sarcasm.

My lawyer was right, though. I am a sucker. It's not compassion, it's codependent compulsion.

58

My lawyer sighed. "Legally," he said, "with parental consent, she can cross state lines. But when you get yourself embroiled in this psychological crap, don't come crying to me."

"Don't worry," I said, "you're not exactly Mr. Compassion."

I like my lawyer and he likes me. Our relationship is built on mutual crankiness. We are both brutally honest and no bullshit. He is one of the most ethical men I have ever met. We make an odd team, but once we got together, we were a smashing success.

I spent the rest of the evening trying to get an apartment set up for Stacie. It was obvious she had to leave her hometown. I didn't want her being taunted. I called everyone I knew and gave the sales pitch. "Look, she's a kid, she was raped, she is going to come up here and I need someone to be with her twenty-four/seven, her mother can't come, she's got four other kids," et cetera, et cetera. You should know, at this point, that I was certain many, many people would volunteer to house her. Friends, family, anyone who heard the tale. Who could resist it? Turns out everyone could. No was the reply I got, time after time. Even my brother Eddie, who I was sure would say yes, said no. For some this would have been the end of the road; for me, it was just a speed bump. I felt nervous but energized. I had to get this done, I could get this done, I would do it. No doubt. Meanwhile, my own little ones were flocking around me. Parker said, "Mom, this is vacation . . . why are you always on the phone?" That was a very good question.

By eleven that night I had it all arranged. I had decided my apartment was the right one. Of course, it was so simple, so easy, I wasn't going to be using it, I would be in Miami by then. I needed a baby-sitter. I got my friend Heidi to quit her job and agree to come stay with Stacie through the last weeks of her pregnancy. In return, I would pay her well. I know how crazy this sounds. Writing it out now—well, it's so embarrassing, I have to fight the urge to hit delete.

At last I fell into bed, exhausted. The phone rang at 4 A.M. It was Stacie.

"Ummm Rosie . . . hi. I don't wanna be no bother," Stacie said.

"Hey, no problem," I said. "I was gonna call you in the morning. Listen, I was thinking maybe it would be easier if you're away until the baby is born."

Stacie started to cry. "This is all my fault," she said. "I'm sorry."

"It is not your fault, and you have nothing to be sorry for." I told her this over and over, over and over, and the night kept coming on.

CHAPTER 10

Dreams

I dream. I dream of a tree outside my window. It is an apple tree but the apples are all rotten. They fall to the ground with black spots on them. They ooze on the pavement and flies come. The tree haunts me. A man climbs up. Branches scrape against my windowsill. Scrape, scrape. They sound like fingernails, or fangs. "Cut down the tree," I cry to my mother and she tries, but she has only a pair of tiny sewing scissors, and so she can't even begin to tackle the trunk.

I dream. Of Angelina Jolie, again. She is in trouble, someone is looking for her, she needs to hide. I want to hide her but I am afraid I will be caught. She tells me not to be a wimp. I don't want to be a wimp, so I listen to her. I hide her in the haunted tree outside my house, the one my mother tried to cut down. She is not afraid of the tree; she thanks me and falls asleep.

I dream. I dream of a building in the gray. Small windows lined up, next to each other, every few feet. The sound of guns, loud bangs, as sparks illuminate the open space behind the men. More gray, endless gray. Noise, chaos. Men.

CHAPTER 11

What do I know about this kid? Why is she so ever-present in my mind, in my day? She is at once here and not. Facts. I grab for facts when reason evades me. I wrote down all I knew.

She is fourteen.

She is pregnant.

She has been raped.

She loves: 'NSYNC, Ricky Martin, her brothers.

She is shy and smart. Tired and troubled. Scared and scarred.

She needs comfort, help, understanding, someone to talk to, her childhood back.

She wants me to help her.

I want to help her.

She needs to place her child, to have it all erased.

She sounds afraid.

She reminds me of me.

I like thinking I can save her, make it all a bit
better.

I know everything happens for a reason.

I wonder where this is going.

I worry I am becoming obsessed.

Obsession, on the whole, has worked for me.

CHAPTER 12

Well, it's not as bad as the Coopers.

I don't remember how many there were; at least four, maybe six. They lived around the block, down by the sump, near the sleigh-riding hill with the high-tension wires that everyone thinks are harmless. Don't believe it. You buy a house for three reasons: location, location, location. Theirs sucked, sucked, sucked.

Mark Cooper was in my grade, kinda small and very cute. Huck Finn meets Michael J. Fox. He wasn't very popular, and he wasn't very clean. In fact, he smelled really bad. (This coming from me, a kid who took a bath maybe once a week.) One morning Mark and I were hanging by our knees, upside down, side by side, in the tiny tree by the sidewalk in front of my house. We were discussing Scooby-Doo and skateboards, lizards and lemonade. The whole time I was thinking, *Mark does smell bad. Maybe he is sick.*

I was good at smelling sickness, disease, and decay. It reeked from my nana's bedroom, closed windows, and unwashed skin. It lay in the living room, covering my mother, sticky sweat and Jean Nate.

It wasn't Mark who was sick, it turned out, it was his mother. She died of something so odd and rare they named it after her. I learned, years later, that their house had no running water for well over a year. The kids, all four or six of them, had to use the bathtub as a toilet. There was no place to wash your face or hair, even if you wanted to.

When Mrs. Cooper got really sick "they" found out. And "they" did whatever it is "they" do when something like "that" happens. The Coopers were gone, all of them, vanished. Mark never finished junior high school. They disappeared and, soon after, their house did too. Condemned by the board of condemners. One morning, with the neighbors looking on, "they" tore it down. There was nothing left of it, at all.

No one ever discussed the Coopers.
Their house.
The way they must have suffered.

When I rode my bike past the vacant lot that was once their home, I would think of the Cooper kids. Each of them a hero. Veterans of an unspoken war too many of us had to fight. I should have been nicer to Mark Cooper. I should have known. *I should have* is going to kill me one day.

The thing about having such desperate horror live right down the block from you, it redefines suffering for all who know the tale. It allows any behavior judged to be even mildly better than theirs to be permissible by comparison. No matter what happened in our house, no matter how badly I felt, how unloved, scared, valueless, someone always answered me with, "Well, it's not as bad as the Coopers."

An eight-word slam dunk, verbal checkmate, conversation over. The Coopers were swamp people.

CHAPTER 13

All are hatched—none just born
Look the same—don't belong

Darkness lingers—beneath skin
Hallow haunted—others' sins

Try to hide—run away
Shower off—dirt and clay

Futile tries—all can see
Others who—are just like we

Safe in the damp—cruel and cold
Young and scared—even when old

See and nod—in passing try
To hold a glance—with fractured eyes

Few make it out—most never do
I'm a swamp person—are you?

CHAPTER 14

I hate my body. I always have. I hate to admit this fact, but it is just that: a fact. I do not look in mirrors, I try never to be naked. If I could have sex with my clothes on I would. I am the dieting queen, but, along with all the other four billion diet queens in this country, I never stick with the program. The highest I've ever gone is 230 pounds, the lowest 160, which for me is skinny. At 160 I feel 230, at 230 I become invisible to myself, just a big piece of bloat. What happens is this: Eventually I'll come across a photo of myself—a shocking experience, have no doubt—and I will demand to know why no one told me of my expanding girth. I need other people's eyes. I cannot see myself; it is impossible.

Except for once. Once, I dated someone with an eating disorder, a dedicated carrot-chomper, and for the short time we were together, I arrived in my own body. She forced me there. She insisted I go to the gym with her twice a day. Pounds started dropping off me as I increased the StairMaster's speed, upped the incline on the treadmill. Afterward we'd share some tofu, as a reward. It was, I see now, a little obsessive, but love or its close facsimile can make you crazy. So I went a little crazy, while, at the same time, flesh just melted and my muscles emerged. The funny thing is, I barely noticed. I was too busy trying to convince my anorexic love of her talent and self-worth. I had no time to see me. Perfect.

The story goes on. I then got invited, by some fluke of fate, to Donald and Marla Trump's wedding. I owned only sweatpants and biker shorts. A fashionable friend took pity on me and dragged me to Barneys. I stayed in the dressing room as she made the saleswoman work. Before I knew it, I was the proud owner of three new Armani suits, all size ten. *Size ten?* I was in shock; I hadn't been size ten since eighth grade. What the hell was going on? I went directly to Baskin Robbins and ordered a waffle cone with two scoops of mint chocolate chip ice cream.

Life is complicated. In the soap opera version I would stay thin forever, rejoicing in my tight tummy, fall in love, and have sex under a waterfall in the noonday sun while Enya blasted on an unseen stereo. Fact is, I missed my old body, the very one I loathed. Fat is a protector; anyone can tell you that. I didn't like being "thin." I felt like people could come too close. When my brief relationship fizzled, so did my trips to the gym, along with my toned, trim body. What a relief.

When I was twenty-nine, I fell in love with a man who was sweet and funny and kinder than any man I had ever known. Tall, blond, and handsome, with a stunning smile, we spoke about getting married, which was both thrilling and repulsive. He didn't care what size my body was and no matter how hard he tried to convince me of that, I never believed him. As he and I got closer, I got bigger. For every pound I gained, I took one step backward, using flesh for padding. I bubble-wrapped my heart.

I am difficult to love, and I know it. I never learned the unconditional part, so trust evades me. Add sex and I fall apart, eventually retreating back into the swamp. Very few people can put up with me, and I can't blame them. I am a constant contradiction. I annoy myself.

• • •

Stacie was arriving in New York City in just two weeks. Heidi was set to baby-sit/live with her. I asked her to stock up the place with healthy kid food and with books that had been favorites of mine when I was her age, Dell paperbacks and Judy Blumes and a book called *Choices,* kind of like a survival manual for teens. I bought new Laura Ashley sheets with those flowers on them, so it would be like sleeping in a meadow, or a country cottage garden. I wanted Stacie to feel safe. I wanted her to feel some sweetness in a life that had been just the opposite.

As for Stacie, she was calling every night now—okay, more than that. Three, four times a night. That's weird, I know. You might want to stop reading right now. It's gonna get kinda creepy.

Our conversations were growing darker, more intense. She was scared, afraid to give birth, afraid of the dark, afraid to sleep. Memories were coming back to her fast and furious, things she knew yet didn't. I mostly listened. I let her talk, because real healing can only come when the mind has opened its floodgates. The rape, it turned out, had been brutal. A little at a time, a little at a time. Stacie began to tell me the things she wished to forget.

I'd listen, trying to make my voice as calm as possible, but I didn't feel calm. I felt a nameless fear, like a cold breeze blowing right through me. Other times I'd get an odd disconnected sense, as though we were in a bad movie and weren't real at all. There were cameras filming us; we had rehearsed these lines; we would be a box office hit. It would all be over when the curtain closed. This was life, however, and the curtain wouldn't close. After our conversations, I'd fall asleep, sometimes at dawn, and have vivid dreams of chickens and chimneys, of Halloween and horror.

I was an abused kid. This is something I have chosen not to dwell on in my public life. It sounds trite, like an *ET* sound bite. But sometimes you can't escape a cliché, and when you can't, you have to go straight to the heart of it and hope there's something not stale at its center. So, yes, I had been abused, although the details are not important. What is important is that I had, supposedly, dealt with the fallout in therapy. How naive I was. Abuse is an ongoing saga for everyone who has lived through it (hence my relationship with Stacie). It may start and stop in real time, but in mind-time it goes on forever.

Why was I drawn to Stacie? Oh, a million reasons, one of which was this: a reliving. A sense of shared pain. Talking to her, I felt this pain, my pain, all over and over again. And although it's hard to admit, I liked how it felt. Electric current, real. It made me feel alive, raw, and sad. I am a swamp person, and so was Stacie.

• • •

As a child I was afraid of just about everything. I grew up in the 1970s, the era of disaster movies. There was always a movie about some earthquake, or the towering inferno, or the sinking ship, or the shark that munched on human limbs. I saw none of those movies. I stayed home and listened to Barry Manilow while my classmates were being chased by Chuckie. What did I need with still more fear? Even the street scared me. There were always all these cars, red cars as shiny as cough drops and cars with fins on them and smacking windshield wipers. I couldn't cross the street without a grown-up watching me, making sure I made it home alive.

How can a child be so scared and saucy at the same time? I was both.

Once, on TV, I watched Saigon fall. I saw the evacuation, all these suffering masses, children streaming down roads, a river of human mud. The last planes were leaving, people climbed over each other in order to get on, to be saved, to live. A young teenage boy, scared and desperate, kicked an old woman off the push-up ladder as she was about to climb aboard. Sacrificing her, saving himself. The old woman fell out of the TV frame, down to the crisis she was running from. I cried and cried. My dad came into the playroom and asked me why I was crying. "Daddy, she was so close, this woman, she had almost made it," I sobbed. He stood confused, my father, looking at the TV, at this child he gave birth to, an animal so unlike himself. I cried and cried and my desperate dad finally turned off the television and said loudly, in a Captain von Trapp voice, "From now on, Roseann, you are not to watch the news. Go to your room."

My favorite place was Jackie's house. We have been best friends since 1965. Her mother, Mrs.

Ellard, had everything: Dixie Riddle Cups and single-sized bags of Fritos, Cool Whip and serving spoons. The place was always so spotless, unlike our house, which was a wreck. Mrs. Ellard's daughters had clean hair and slick-straight parts that showed the pink seams of their scalps. As for my own hair, it was so full of tangles one time the school nurse cut the knots out of it. I told my dad the Ellards had a special spray called No More Tangles, and that it came in a white bottle. I needed it. He never bought it. He had a dead wife and five small kids; no more tangles was not a priority. It was to me.

• • •

As Stacie began calling more and more, I began to sleep less and less. A sane person would have sensed that the "relationship" was totally unhealthy, and not serving either one of us. But I didn't realize it. I explained the whole thing to myself under that rubric *help*. The girl needed help, I love to help. I am a very good helper. It's good to help, right?

I have wondered and wondered what giving help means to me, why I am so pulled toward impulsive generosity. Part of it is probably normal enough: I have more money than I need, and there are people out there who don't have enough. They, too, have been through things no one should be forced to endure, and they need help putting the pieces back together. I can give that help, so I do. Swamp people stick together.

But it's more than that. Over and over again I find myself struggling in crazy situations where people ask for more and more and I keep shoving out my hand, saying, "Here! Here! Here!" with plain desperation in my voice. Why?

Maybe it's a girl thing. As women, we are taught early on that our greatest worth in the world is how we can soothe. Maybe it's also an abuse thing. When your boundaries have been violated, you just plain and simple stop *seeing* the space between people, so people's pain becomes your pain and you have to stop it. At the same time, though, codependency is also a distancing ploy; you're so busy trying to save the world out there you forget about the people close to you, and then, last of all, or first of all, you forget about yourself, that you might be the one worth saving.

By now all my friends and family knew about Stacie and my midnight madness. Frankly, they were scared. They each tried, unsuccessfully, to convince me I was in over my head. I told them they were idiots, uncaring, selfish, frightened cowardly idiots. My friend Carolyn, who routinely beats me at Scrabble, told me to knock it off. "Sounds weird, Ro." What did she know of weird? Carolyn, with her Ivy League education, was definitely not a swamp person. I listened to her spiel and said, "Uh-huh, whatever." I am known for my snappy retorts.

One evening Carolyn came over for dinner. We did the usual, ate, played Scrabble, and then talked friend to friend. The phone rang; I let the machine pick up. It was Stacie.

"Rosie, umm, it's Stacie, I ummm, well, I will call back."

The silence between Carolyn and me felt forever. Finally she said, "You know Ro, I love you, and your big heart, but I don't believe her."

"What part don't you believe?"

"All of it. Let me hear the message again," she said.

So I played it again, mostly to shut her up. I had saved the last few messages, so there were a bunch to hear. I picked up the phone and hit the speaker button. I followed the prompts. First there was Barb's voice, from earlier in the day. "Rosie," she said into the tape, "I want to thank you for . . ." Then there was another message from Doug, Stacie's father, who at his wife's urging had finally begun to speak with me. "Look Rosie," he said, "just tell us to bug off. There's no way we're not overwhelming you."

"Okay," said Carolyn, "so where's Stacie?"

Suddenly, after hearing Doug's message, she appeared highly interested.

"Next," I said. I flipped to the next recording. There was the meek sweet sound of Stacie. Carolyn nodded in a noncommittal way. The tape

79

ended. There was a long pause. I couldn't see my friend's face—she was turned away from me, looking into my living room—but I could practically feel her thinking through something.

"What is it?" I said.

"I don't know," Carolyn said. "To tell you the truth, Ro, she doesn't really sound like a kid."

"Since when are you an expert on kids?" I said.

"I'm just telling you what I think," said Carolyn.

"Well, how do you think a raped fourteen-year-old *should* sound?" I asked.

"Look," said Carolyn. "I am just gonna say this once, the whole story, the rape, the pregnancy, don't you think it's all a little melodramatic?"

"Of course I do," I snapped. "Life is melodramatic, Carolyn. Let's drop it."

"Ro," she said. "There's no way for you to know if this 'kid' is telling the truth."

"God, Strauss, you are acting like she is a convicted felon."

"She could be a felon, or an adult. You know, all three of those voices sound sort of like the same person to me."

Was Carolyn kidding me? She had to be kidding. I waited for the smile. It never came.

"You're serious? Come on, why would Stacie lie?" I asked. "There's no reason. She has not asked for money, neither has her mom, they won't even call collect. She isn't lying."

"You can't know that, Ro," Carolyn said.

80

"I know," I said. "This kid's been beaten, abused, and now you're not believing her? The worst thing you can do to a victim is doubt them."

"But some victims," said Carolyn, "are doubtful. Some victims aren't victims. They're people starving for attention."

"You don't know anything," I stated.

"Just think about it, Ro."

I nodded and told myself I would not. Carolyn knew nothing about swamps, at all. This much was clear.

• • •

Stacie called that night in a panic. Tommy Gonzales, the rapist's five-year-old son, the boy Stacie used to baby-sit for, had called her a few moments before. The boy asked Stacie why she made his daddy go away. Stacie was inconsolable.

"Did you tell your mom and dad? You have to tell them," I said.

"I did," Stacie said.

"Did they tell the police?"

"Yeah," Stacie said. Now her voice was flat, like roadkill.

"Don't fade out on me, Stace," I said. "We can make them stop calling your house . . . and . . ."

"And what," said Stacie, suddenly, shockingly snide, "what . . . are you gonna tell me that I'll be all the stronger for it? That God will bless me when I get to heaven's gates? Screw that," Stacie said. "There ain't no God."

"I don't know, Stacie," I said, and I didn't. The kid had a point. Just turn on the evening news. Kids raze bullets through schools, and parents identify dead kids through dental records. Corpses are shoveled into ovens, and then, decades later, people deny it ever happened. Planes go down while passengers scream. Mothers just drop dead, their cells all rusted, and scary mystery men climb trees at midnight. Kids can't cross the street alone, Etan Patz was still missing, Daytwon Bennett was dead, mysterious murders, perpetrators everywhere. . . .

"Don't fade out on me Ro," Stacie said, her voice turning adultlike. It was amazing how fast we switched places, the caring and the cared for. . . .

"Listen, I am sorry," I said.

"Yeah, me too," Stacie said.

• • •

The worst thing, the absolute worst thing, is to have to do my show when I'm depressed. Since I have been depressed for a long time, I know how to dance around it. My job is to be happy and funny; when I'm not I just go on autopilot. Usually that works well enough. But it gets so tiring, having to pretend, the mask tied tightly to my real face. Then again, what is my real face? Would I even recognize it in the mirror?

I did my show the next day feeling down, wondering where God was. I had an afternoon meeting with the suits. "Look," I said to them, "thanks for the offer, the show has been amazing for me in ways I cannot explain, but I'm telling you right now, I'm not renewing my contract."

No one believed me. No one even listened. "We will come up with a better offer. People don't walk away from that kind of money, Rosie," they said, laughing.

"Well," I said, "I've got more than I'll ever need. And besides, this isn't about money."

That is a sentence rarely uttered in the land of showbiz. There was a stunned silence. Everyone looked toward me.

"Well then, what is it about?" someone asked.

"It's about . . . it's about . . . the show is not me, or all of me. There are pieces of me I can't express on my show. And it's not even that, really, it is just, that, it is hard to explain."

No reaction, at all.

I steadied myself. "I know it is not what you want to hear, but this show. It's not real."

"What is real?" Jim said.

I didn't have an answer.

The conversation ended with "Rosie, we are talking millions of dollars." As if that were the only real factor.

I couldn't find a way to express it to them. I

had thought this life, fame and money, would bring me solace, inner peace, happiness. I thought the bad stuff would become good, and the good stuff, amazing. I imagined salvation, as I clawed my way up. And having arrived there, without feeling what I expected to, I found myself in need of a new destination. The life I am living feels like a movie, and I have been miscast.

I thought maybe I would do a magazine. I didn't tell a lot of people. It wasn't a secret, but it wasn't a done deal by any means, so there wasn't much to tell. My business managers and lawyers came up with the initial concept. I thought, *Maybe*. I'd always admired writers. I'd always loved words on a page. Somehow, words seemed to bypass image and get straight to the heart of things. Somehow, words seemed big enough to contain pain, and sentences could pull broken bits together.

That evening, after my show, I walked home, which is unusual for me to do. This was the summer of the West Nile virus, the summer of rodents and trash, just ten days before I would get to go to Miami, my place of bliss. A strange thing happened on the walk home. No one said hello to me, and I found a tiny child's shoe, a nearly new white shoe, just lying sideways on the sidewalk. I picked it up. There is nothing quite so haunting as a miniature shoe or mitten strewn on the street, its tiny occupant unknown. I held it in my hand. I lifted its leather tongue and peered inside it, and there, I saw all these stars swim.

That night, when the phone rang, I said, "Stace, I gotta tell you—" and then the voice that came back at me was not Stacie's. "It's Barb," she said. "Stacie's begun to bleed. They think her blood pressure is too high, preeclampsia something. She's in the hospital. I'm calling from the hospital."

"Jesus," I said, "will she be okay?" I looked at my caller ID. It was a different number.

There was a long pause on the line. "I don't know," Barb said.

"Can I talk to her?"

"No, she is out of it," Barb said, ". . . she's very weak."

"Okay," I said. I felt fear grip me.

"The doctor looks worried. . . ." Her voice trailed off as she started to cry.

That's all it took. I donned my superhero attire in a flash. I sprang into action.

"Listen, if you need anything, need me to talk to the doctors, or to her, if you want to call, whenever, whatever. . . ." I was rambling, just rambling, codependent compulsive mumbo-jumbo.

"Hey," I continued, "maybe when this is all over you and Stacie can come down to Miami for a weekend, I have a lot of free mileage tickets . . . it could be fun . . . or I could come over and visit you both." I pictured myself riding into town, saving this little girl's reputation, her dignity, her childhood. Saving maybe myself.

"I could make you my famous meat loaf," Barb said.

"That sounds great," I said, even though I hate meat loaf. I saw myself sitting at a kitchen table with checkered curtains and whipped white mashed potatoes.

"Can I talk to her?" I asked again.

Barb paused. Then she said, "Hold on."

Three, maybe four minutes passed. When you're on TV, doing a show, there is little silence. You have to talk fast, and you have to keep your guests going. We put Yodels and cupcakes on the audience's seats, to get them sugared up, so they laugh and clap. Silence on television is not allowed. In it, anything unscripted can happen.

Now I listened to the silence on the line. It terrified me. It also felt pure and true. I trembled. Silence is the loudest sound of all. It hums and whirs. At last, a tiny voice.

"Hi Rosie." Her breathing was ragged.

"You okay, Stace?" I asked.

"I have, like, no breath," Stacie said, and indeed, she sounded that way.

"You know," said Stacie, her voice sounding smaller and smaller, "I really wish you were here with me."

"I do too," I said, and I did. I pictured her hospital room, the chrome bed, the bars, her head with its blondish hair uncombed; it felt so real but, of course, it wasn't. I was not there, I was not even close.

CHAPTER 15

Spingles; spine tingles.

Twin brothers, both survived a house of horrors, a cold cruel childhood full of beatings and bruises. A hurtful hate-filled past that tore them apart inside, and from each other. One brother goes on to be the CEO of a Fortune 500 company. He does not see or think of his family of origin. He has created a new family, with a loving wife and happy children. A life rife with hope and health. His twin, however, has not been as lucky. He is in jail, on death row. His last wish is to see his twin, once more.

Through a thick Plexiglas barrier, over crackling phone lines, the brothers stare at each other. Silence. A guard taps the prisoner on the shoulder, telling him visiting hour is almost over. The convicted man looks across the scratched window and sees his own face in a business suit staring back at him. Finally he speaks.

"After all we suffered, how could you succeed?" he asks.

The twin loosens his tie, takes a deep breath, and answers him, "After all we suffered, how could you not?"

CHAPTER 16

One night, after a particularly unsettling Stacie conversation, I found an old movie on cable TV. I don't remember the title, or the stars, but the sizzle crawled up my back and zinged my heart.

A boat had sunk, a luxury liner. There was only one lifeboat left floating. In it were twenty-four people, some clinging to the sides, some sitting on the edge, as the boat was built for only ten. The oldest member of the crew was a young man in his early twenties. He was in charge, like it or not, by virtue of his rank alone. Without enough food or water, this man/boy had to make harrowing decisions. To save any, he had to sacrifice some. It pained him, but he did what he had to do. He ended up saving twelve people, including himself, while losing as many to the sea. He placed those who were sick, too old, unable to hang on any longer, in life jackets and re-

91

leased them into the waves. No one stopped him. Few questioned his decisions. All were in crisis, none wanted to be him.

So they were saved, these eleven, who owed their very lives to the courage and character in this young man. He led them to safety. Once on dry land, however, things changed, perspectives shifted. The eleven who lived turned on the one who saved them.

The man/boy/officer was brought up on charges of murder. Each wounded survivor, unable to deal with the knowledge that they had lived and their loved ones had not, pointed fingers and assigned blame urgently, as if to erase their own. The man, the victim, the hero, the leader, was found guilty of killing those he had not saved.

Spingle.

We are both the saved and released. We are at once the victors and the failed, to and of each other. All of us, strangers, friends, and siblings. We are all connected.

Spingles. Follow their path down impulse lane, dig and dig and find their origin. Nothing happens by chance.

CHAPTER 17

I have many regrets.

Halloween 1974. It was seven at night, almost dark, still safe for trick-or-treating as long as you weren't alone. I was twelve, the oldest of our costume-clad crowd. We were sitting on the El-lards' lawn, me, my sister Maureen, and my baby brother Timmy. He must have been seven. We were stuffing our mouths with the night's bounty when I saw them making their way toward us, the Rita Crescent kids. They scared me. Rebels, little tough-talking twerps who smoked pot and cut out of school. Leading the pack was Drew Ober, the king of cool. In his hand were some raw eggs. He caught my eye, Drew Ober, and asked me if he could egg my brother.

He actually asked me, "Can I egg your brother?" I was shocked that Drew Ober was talk-ing to me. It took me no time to answer.

I said yes.

I said yes, and when I did, Drew Ober threw an egg at my baby brother Timmy. He hit him square in the back, on the first try. Then Drew and his band of assholes walked away laughing.

We went home, me, Maureen, and Timmy. There was a large raised, red welt on Timmy's back where the egg had hit him. I put some ice on it. Timmy never cried. I did.

Regret. Severe. Extreme. Painful. Pure. Regret.

"No you cannot egg my brother, you pothead moron!" That's the sentence that played in my mind for months in a continuous loop. Yes is what I said, no is what I meant; by twelve it was an established pattern. I went from victim/protector to villain/perpetrator with one little word. Yes. I hated myself for it.

It still fills me with shame, thirty years later.

I told Timmy this guilt-filled tidbit at a family wedding last year. I waited till we were both fairly toasted to do it. He stared at me for a moment, his face morphing into the baby boy he once was as I waited for his response. I was ready for anything he was going to say. He said nothing, he just laughed. He thought I was joking; he was waiting for a punch line that never came. I made it clear that I was not kidding. I was deeply sorry I had betrayed him all those years ago. He laughed again, long and hard. He told me he did not remember anything about the incident at all. He told me to forget about it, and he went to the bar to get us another drink. While he did I replayed each detail.

The sweet sticky smell of candy apples.
The brisk windy night.
Smiles and laughter.
Gumdrops and Hershey Kisses.
Shaving cream and chalk-filled socks.
And then Drew Ober.

"NO YOU CANNOT EGG MY BROTHER!"

I went to Rita Crescent only once. My stomach tightened and my heart began to race as I hopped the Nordins' fence and saw them. Surely they would send me away, see me for the fake that I was. They would sense my innate nerdy nature and banish me back to Rhonda Lane. Nope, no one noticed me. They continued "hanging out," rolling joints, drinking beer, and being "cooler" than I ever could in my entire life. A girl in bare feet and a halter top had a piece of chalk. She was writing the names of all the "Rita" gang on the street, in columns. I was listed under MAYBE. It both thrilled and sickened me. Someone lit up a joint and passed it in my direction. I ran home as fast as I could.

I knew all about the dangers of drugs. Nana told me about Art Linkletter's daughter at least twice a week. "Now dolly, you know what happened to Art Linkletter's daughter, right? Such a sin what she did to that family. She ruined everything by doing the drugs, it all starts with the pot. First they take the pot, then the heroin, then the LSD. Next thing you know they are jumping out the window like she did. Right out the window, dead. Poor Art Linkletter."

I knew I would never be a Rita Crescent girl.

I saw Drew Ober a few months after Halloween in Baracini's candy store. I pretended not to notice him. It didn't work. "I've seen better faces on a clock . . ." he began; the rest is a blur. I knew right then, as I paid for my chocolate-covered cherries, that I had invited this torment. That in some way my allowing him to hurt my brother made it okay for him to hurt me too. We walked out, Maureen and I, without acknowledging his existence, or each other's pain. A trick we had mastered.

Lying in the way, way back of the new used green station wagon, crying silently, I said, "Come on, Bessie," loud enough for all to hear. Then familiar silence.

CHAPTER 18

I used to hurt myself a lot. Skinned knees, broken bones, assorted scratches and scrapes. It is hard to explain, embarrassing to admit, but I liked getting injured. I liked the pain, and then I liked the getting tended to. One time I took a bottle cap and bent it down the middle. I was alone, my mom was dead, I was feeling everything and nothing at once. I held the pinched metal disc in my hand and started to slowly run it back and forth over my forearm. I wasn't looking at the mark it was making; I wasn't feeling anything, just more of the same numbness that had settled in after her funeral—the dead zone. So I am rubbing and thinking about Patty Hearst, who was kidnapped and now robbing banks in California. About having to go back to school where everyone would know I had a dead mother. About getting my period, and how horrible that was going to be with just a dad. My dad. I moved the bent bottle cap; it tingled, almost pleasant. I felt a raindrop on my leg. I looked up to a cloudless sky. Then another drop, I looked down, and saw it was my arm. I was a bloody mess, red, vibrant, alive, and flowing. I ran into my house. My dad was at work, my siblings out playing with friends. It was just me. I went upstairs and washed the cuts out with the bubbly stuff Mrs. Ellard always used; I found some Band-Aids, and Neosporin; I put them on too. Then I was finished, all cared for and cleaned up.

My wounds became words; they screamed out what could not be spoken. The pain on the outside reflected the pain on the inside. I felt one with myself, finally.

One summer I put my arm through the garage window. We were roller skating, I needed to stop, I had a choice: the glass window or the wood ledge. I chose the glass. I was bloody, but I didn't care. I plucked out the big pieces, then ran out of the dark garage and into my mother's rock garden, where I danced around in the sweet stink of flowers.

CHAPTER 19

Stacie got better in one way, worse in another. Her physical condition stabilized and her blood pressure went down to normal. That was the good news. The bad news was that her mind was going kerphooey and by the time the medical team had finished doing what they needed to do with the fetal heart monitors and the IV drips, she was mute, and staring, rocking back and forth. Her mother was a mess; she could hardly speak when she called, overwhelmed with worry.

They transferred Stacie to the hospital's psych ward. Barb said it was a good ward, but to my mind, how can a psych ward be good for a pregnant fourteen-year-old kid? I asked Barb if they could just keep her in the maternity wing. She said she had asked and was told no. I pictured her, little Stacie, up on the seventh floor with troubled scary-looking adults all around her. Little Stacie, on her twin bed, her belly bulging.

I couldn't stop thinking about her. I was wishing her, willing her to talk, from two thousand miles away. I sent her a phone card, Beanie Babies, word search books. I couldn't shake her, this kid I had never met, like a button in my brain was permanently pressed, bing, bing, bing, her face, bing bing bing, her voice, bing bing bing, what can I do to help?

I thought about flying there to see her. I thought about it a lot, swooping down like Mighty Mouse, in the nick of time. If I did, she would talk to me, I was sure. She would see me, and come out of it, and be better. Yes, that's what would have happened if I flew there. I never did. Why? Many reasons. I worried it would be a big scene, with me there in that tiny hospital, in that tiny town. I worried that I would be intruding, that it wasn't my place. I worried about my sanity, leaving my own kids to fly across the country to meet a kid I did not know.

So, Stacie is in a psych ward, and I am talking to her mom, Barb. Nothing much happens. She is still not talking. I am still obsessing. Friends are still worrying. I look off into space, they ask, "What are you thinking about?" and I say *Stacie*. It got so embarrassing that I started to make up things so they wouldn't think I was nuts. Which I was starting to think I was.

I began to feel tired, pale-faced. One morning

I woke up after a particularly disturbing dream and decided to decoupage. I did an entire toy box. It took me seven hours. I had to finish it. Layer after layer of glued paper, overlapping, peeking out, corners here, a hint there. A splash of red, some green in the back. The smell of the glue, the varnish, the sticky hands, the dirty T-shirt. I needed it. You can tell how stressed I am by how many completed pieces I have in my craft room. I like making something from nothing, going from scrapped to saved. What some see as junk, I see as potential. A yard sale and some Mod Podge, life manageable.

I finished. It was beautiful, but it wasn't enough. I wanted comfort. I went to the movies, alone. It is always embarrassing to say "one" to the woman in the ticket booth. She hands me my ticket with a mixture of surprise and pity.

Ummmmmm I have a lot of friends, but I just needed to get out of my house in a rush, 'cause there is this pregnant kid, and I worry about her all the time, and she isn't talking, and I want to fix it all for her, but I can't, so I crafted, and still felt IT, that IT that can swallow you, so I just drove here, and I don't really wanna see this movie, but it is the only one playing anytime soon, even though I have forty-five minutes before it starts. . . .

That's what I was thinking, but I said nothing. I just smiled, and while waiting for the movie, I walked through the mall and into the nature store.

It was a very soothing New Age store where tiny fountains splashed over sculpted rocks and wind chimes chimed in the fan's breeze. The woman behind the counter was plump. I liked her right away. Usually New Age people bug me; they have no humor. Not today, though. This woman had crystal bracelets on, and she smelled of Egyptian musk. I went up to her. I said, "Whaddya have for nerves?"

She said, "Are you getting all your B vitamins? They're important for the nervous system."

I said, "I take a multi every day. . . . I was thinking more like, magic."

She smiled. "Magic?"

"Yep," I said.

"Rosie?" she asked.

"Yep," I answered.

The problem with fame: no anonymity. When you ask for "magic" at a store that doesn't sell tricks, being famous sucks.

"Stones," the woman said, "we have these peace stones, and when you hold them and rub your thumb over the words engraved in them, they bring a balance to your life."

"Lemme see them," I said.

She grabbed a tray from the glass case and asked, "Why is your life unbalanced?"

You know you are in trouble when the saleswoman at the nature store asks you a question that almost makes you cry. I bit the inside of my mouth.

I said, "I'm having a lot of . . . dreams." I added, "Bad dreams."

"Oh, the stones should help," she said. "Put them beneath your pillow at night and they'll release positive energy."

I touched the stones. They were cool and smooth, veined with white, and they did send something soothing into my fingers. "I'll take 'em," I said.

"Which ones?" she asked.

"All," I said.

"Those must be some serious dreams," she said, ringing them up.

"You have no idea."

I left the store and went to see the movie. When I got home, I put the stones under my pillow, beneath my mattress, at the foot of my bed, at the threshold of doors; I slept on the stones, and you know what? They didn't work.

Dreams

I am running in a field; again the gray building in the distance. It stands maybe ten feet high. At the six-foot level is a row of windows. The windows are square, four inches by four inches. Each one holds the barrel of a rifle, and a man, behind, in the darkness. A man I cannot see. I hear the shots, I see the flashes of orange-yellow-blue. They are firing at me, and I am running.

103

Always running, looking toward the building and then not. I must run, keep running, before they get me.

I am lost, in a strange city. I don't like to travel, I am panicked. There are neon lights everywhere, raisins fall from open windows. Old women walk with their heads down, scurrying, frantic. I see Angelina Jolie. She is selling apples.

I am an adult, in my house, it doesn't look like my house. Water is coming in from every open surface. It is quite clear I am about to drown.

So much for magic stones.

• • •

I sent Stacie more and more presents. Barb told me she wasn't doing well. She was catatonic a lot of the time, and when she wasn't catatonic she was crying. Barb said she wouldn't be coming to New Jersey to give birth, there was no way she'd be well enough. She'd probably have the baby right there, in the psych ward. God, the poor kid. I waited for her to call.

I came down with a bad cold. It was July by then, the heat suffocating, and my sinuses filled with wet cement. My head throbbed. My fever spiked and dipped and spiked again. I remember taking a red decongestant and wishing it was winter. I was very tired.

Carolyn came over. We were watching a movie, chatting about life. She told me she was worried about me. "Hey," I said, "it's just a cold. I think you're overreacting."

"Funny," she said, all deadpan and Harvardy. "You know, Ro, I think this Stacie thing is way out of control. It's not right."

"Yeah?" I said. "According to whom?"

"Well, you seem a bit obsessed," Carolyn said.

"Here we go again, it's not an obsession," I said. "She is just a kid, Carolyn."

Carolyn rolled her eyes. "Ro, trust me."

"What do you mean?"

"I'd like to talk with her myself," said Carolyn.

"You are out of luck, she doesn't have to prove herself to you," I said. "She has been through enough already."

"How about we call the hospital and see if they have her registered," Carolyn said, condescendingly.

I squinted up at my friend. "Why?"

"If you're so sure this is all true and not some deranged person playing tricks on you, than let me call and verify it. It can't hurt. What hospital's she in?"

"Bournewood," I said, in a tone that let her know I thought she was a moron, an Ivy League moron. "I have the number, I have already called there . . . more than once."

"Okay, so maybe I am paranoid. . . . Call now?" she challenged me.

"If it would make you happy, I'll call," I said, indignant.

Carolyn handed me the phone. I had the number on a Post-it note, somewhere in my address book. I found it. I'd never actually called the hospital before, but I wasn't about to admit that. Why would I call the hospital? I had no reason to. I'd waited for Barb to call me with news. Far away, in a different state, I heard the phone ring and ring and then a click, click. "Bournewood," someone said, "can I help you?"

I hung up fast. I was breathless with anxiety. "Okay," I said. "See, they're not lying. The woman said *Bournewood*. Are you satisfied?"

"But you didn't ask if she was registered there," Carolyn said.

"Come on, Carolyn . . . why would someone pull something like this?"

"Maybe your fame, maybe your money," Carolyn said.

"Maybe not," I said. "I've offered them money. I've offered them phone cards and cash and you name it, and they've refused it all. So there goes that theory. They don't want money, Carolyn. They want help."

CHAPTER 20

On the third day of her psych ward stay, Stacie called. She said, "Rosie, you gotta get me outta here." I wished I could. I knew I couldn't. I changed the subject. "Did you get the Game Boy?" She said, "Yeah, but they took it away."

"But you're talking," I said. "Your mom told me you weren't talking."

"I'm talking now," she said. "I wanna get outta here and have things be like they were before."

"Before when?" I said.

"Just before," she said.

Before it all collapsed. Before it got so very ugly, before it was completely ruined. Before every last piece of me lay in crumbs on the bottom of nowhere.

Because Stacie would be having the baby in Oregon and not near my agency, I called a social work agency in her town. I explained the situation. I said, "This girl is about to deliver, she is fragile, she needs her hand held. I am not sure her mom can do it. I've found adoptive parents but I need someone to do an intake. . . ."

I told Janice, the social worker, the whole story. She said, "It sounds pretty weird, Rosie, have you ever met this girl?"

"No," I said, "but you will on Friday. The mom asked me to set it up. They want to place, they are just scared. Look, it's legit, Janice. Meet her, you will see what I mean."

Janice paused. "Okay," she agreed, "but it sounds weird . . . a rape, a youth minister? Why didn't they report it?"

"They reported it. I know his name, he is in jail," I said.

"Okay," she said slowly, as she took down the details. "How far along did you say she was?"

"Any day," I said. "She's practically at term."

What happened next is a blur in my mind. I spoke to Stacie on the phone at night. I remember, also, speaking to Barb, and then to a nurse by the name of Jolene, who sounded very nurse-like, crisp and confident, with a hint of warmth beneath her busy efficiency. She said, "Stacie's getting better. She's a tough kid, and she will make it."

"Good," I said. "Take extra care of her." Jolene said she would do her best.

*   *   *

I slept, took red decongestants, played with my kids, tried to relax. A day, two, maybe three passed. I looked for signs, pregnant teenagers, 'NSYNC songs, girls named Stacie. I found none. I believe in signs, I need them, I use them as proof. What proof did I want? That she would get better? That she was real? Was I doubting her? I don't think I was. Carolyn tried to plant seeds of doubt in my mind, but I resisted their growth. Her reasoning was all wrong, too logical, too intellectual. I go with my gut. I know stuff. I knew that Stacie was real, that this relationship had meaning. Nothing happens by chance.

So, the blur. It's simple, really, but sometimes the simplest things are the hardest to say. Stacie claimed one morning to me over the phone that she could no longer feel the baby move, hadn't felt it in hours.

"Hours?" I asked.

"Days," she said.

"Go tell the nursing staff," I said. "Right away!"

She did. They cuffed her with a fetal monitor—Barb explained it all to me after the fact—and they got no heartbeat. They did a sonogram and what they saw in there . . . they saw a little dead girl. The umbilical cord was around her neck. "There's no chance for survival," the doctors announced. "The only thing left to do is to get the baby out."

"Give her a C-section," Barb pleaded. "Don't make my daughter go through labor."

Barb was telling me all this after the fact, crying on the phone.

But they couldn't give Stacie a C-section, something about the blood type of the baby, incompatible, didn't want to risk it. They said a vaginal birth would be the only safe way to go.

"You're going to make my daughter give birth to a dead baby?" Barb asked.

Indeed they were. Indeed they did. They put her on pitocin and her uterus went into spasm. She labored for seven hours. I've never had a baby and so I don't know, but I can imagine. I can imagine so many, many things it's sometimes difficult to know what is dream and what is actual history. Kidnapped dead mothers, spy planes, Buster Brown baby shoes, scary midnight men, talking rugs. Stacie's pain was a series of flames. The baby, deflated like an air doll, crowning downward. It came out in a flash of blood, blue, but it was not blue. "No, it was not blue," Barb told me over the phone. "The baby was pink and perfect and I held her. Stacie didn't, though. She didn't want to see her."

The baby, somehow, had retained its color, but that night, in my dream, it was blue. It was denim blue and I split the seam of its eye so I could see inside. I opened the dead baby's eye and I stared deep in, like, long ago, I had stared deep into my mother's eyes as she lay going.

The next morning I called the social worker in Oregon, the one who was just about to leave to meet Stacie and do the intake. I said, "Don't bother. The adoption's off. The baby died."

The social worker paused on the line.

"I don't know how to tell you this," she said.

"Tell me what?"

"There is no baby," she said.

"I know," I said. "The baby died. Last night. Stillborn."

"No," she said. "I mean, there never was a baby. I checked it out for you. There is no record of a pregnant teenager at that hospital. There are no records of a Barb and Doug Davis in Ashland, Oregon, or anywhere in the state. There is no Stacie. I've looked and looked and turned up nothing. I'm sorry, Rosie," she said. "This has all been a hoax."

CHAPTER 21

How can something so real be so fake?
How can something so fake be so real?
How can I love so much and love so little?
How can I have children and yet also be a child?
How is it possible that I am a victim and a victor?
Nothing makes sense.
The world spins and spins.
There are so many broken pieces.
You hang on tight and still, you tip.

CHAPTER 22

Chelsea cannot stop talking about the dead bird. She was in the park, with her brothers, on her way toward the swings and the sandbox. She saw, in her path, on the dirt walkway, a newborn baby bird. A dead newborn baby bird. Chelsea is three, she has the vocabulary of a forty-year-old. She also, I think, has obsessive-compulsive disorder, just like I do. When something gets into her head, it stays there.

"Mama, there was a baby bird, it fell out of its nest, and it was dead. The mommy must have been very sad, I bet, 'cause the baby was gone. Forever. Dead. And it must have fallen out of its nest, where the mother bird put it. Maybe the baby bird was looking for something to eat, or trying to see the sky, and it tipped over the edge. Then it was dead. This baby bird, Mama. And I know the bird's mommy is really very sad."

So we talked for a long time about birds,

mommies, and death. About the fragility of nests as a whole, about sudden sadness, how life can change in a split second. Chelsea asked again about my mother, her grandmother, who is, like the baby bird, quite dead. Was she looking for a safety net? Something to protect her should she unexpectedly begin to free-fall? I wasn't sure, yet I dug out my stories, the ones I had tucked away for special occasions such as this. She sat on my lap as I told her of the World's Fair boat ride. A story she knew by heart, but listened to again, waiting for a new sliver, a hidden gem I had not yet revealed. We went through our usual Q and A.

Why didn't they give my mommy medicine?
Was I very sad?
Who made me lunch?
Did I still miss her?

I answered, as I always do, slightly amazed at my daughter's rawness, her unending emotional access. Then there was a pause. I knew what was coming. Something Parker never asked, something most three-year-olds would not be able to articulate.

"Where is my tummy lady? Is she ever coming to see me?"

I took a breath. I told her I did not know her tummy lady, as she is not in our family. She was not going to come visit, because she knew

Chelsea was with her right mommy now. She was a nice lady, I was sure, because she listened when God told her of the mix-up, that the baby in her tummy was someone else's. The tummy lady loved Chelsea, a lot, I told her.

"I bet she is sad," she said, a little sad herself. Real-life parenting is nothing like sitcoms.

I stroked her blond curls. "Yes, Chels, I bet she was sad, but I think she is okay now. You know, when you are older, you can go meet her, Chelsea, if you want to. I will go with you, if you want me to, because I would like to meet her too. I want to look into her eyes and say thank you. Thank you for listening to God, for knowing that Chelsea belonged in my family, for loving my baby girl so much."

There was silence. Nothing. Just air between us.

"It is very sad when a baby falls out of the nest," she told me with authority. I waited for more. "Mama, you wanna go watch a tape?"

We did, *The Wizard of Oz* as usual. "See Mama, Dorothy's socks are blue, not white." A fact Chelsea brought up to me last Halloween, when I presented her with her Dorothy costume, complete with ruby slippers and white socks. She looked at me, perplexed. "Dorothy wears blue socks on *The Wizard of Oz*, Mama," she said, as if I was a complete moron. I put in the videotape to check and see, and sure enough she was right. "Yes, Chels, her socks *are* blue!" I said, as she

117

held my eyes and nodded. My daughter notices everything.

I realized that night, as I watched her sleep, we have our own safety net, Chelsea and I. Built of Halloween costumes and rewatched movies, of tummy ladies and baby birds. Of all questions allowed, and answers always given.

She is something, my daughter. My mother would have loved her.

CHAPTER 23

There is no Stacie, this has all been a hoax."

I have many names. Ro, Mama, Rosie, O'D, Roseann, dolly; I have so many selves. I am Ro the mom, Roseann the crafter, Rosie the comedian, Roseann the sacred one, Ro the best friend, Rosie the bad friend, Ro the needy, Rosie the giver, Roseann the child, still at almost forty. Now I had yet a new role. Rosie the duped.

"There is no Stacie, this has all been a hoax."

I could not believe it. I did not believe it. If it was a hoax, I was going to get to the bottom of it. But let me say, for the first few hours after the social worker told me there were no records of a birth, no records of a Davis family in Ashland, Oregon, I just lay on my couch. I stared at the ceiling. I kept thinking how funny it was, the plaster up there all in little balls, like cottage cheese.

When things go wrong, when life takes a sudden swerve, I get into gear. After *there is no Stacie, this has all been a hoax* played endlessly in my mind for about an hour, I revved the engines, full speed, no stopping. I would find out what went down, and I would find it out right away. No sleepless night worrying I was a loser, a taken fool, a dupe. I thought, *I should call Carolyn, she'll know what to do,* but I was in no mood for an *I told you so.* Besides, even with the social worker's stunning news, I still knew there was way more to this story. There had to be. I felt it. It was not some sick trick.

Okay. Take action. I paced. I stand when I am enraged, remorseful, joyous. It is like there are too many feelings, I've got to get up and dance with them. Confusion clouded my head. Then I calmly went to my phone, called the police station in Ashland, Oregon, where Stacie and her mom lived. How I was gonna explain this whole thing, I didn't know. I dialed.

"Hi, this is Rosie O'Donnell." I waited.

"From television?" a woman's voice asked.

"Yes." No one ever believes me.

"No way!" she said.

"Way," I said. "Now listen. I have a kinda weird story and I need some information." I gave her the *Reader's Digest* version. "I need to know whether there's a Barb and Stacie Davis in your

120

town and whether they have any criminal record."

"We can't give out that sort of information," she said. "Criminal records are confidential."

"Yeah," I said, "but I need to know."

"Rosie," she said. "I believe you. But I can't give out that information."

So I went on-line, to Yahoo maps. I typed in 7 Hysink Road, Ashland, Oregon, and my hard drive made a grinding sound, like it was searching all its gears, and then, there it was. The map was crude and the directions were piss poor, but it was real; it was *real*. At least the address was there. I was so relieved. I thought, *Okay. Now what?*

I went back on-line. My feelings had stopped. I was totally into action, crime solving, Columbo on crack. I was a hard drive searching its circuits. I typed in Barbara Davis in the question box, and guess what? I got a hit. She did exist. Barbara Davis, in Anaheim, California. So maybe they'd just lied to me about the locale. That was it, it was a locale issue. Had I ever checked whether the area code on my caller ID was Oregon? No, I had not. They didn't want me sending money, they had specifically asked that I not send money, so they were trying to protect me by making up a fake locale. This, I know, is not the most logical thinking in the world, but at the moment it made perfect sense.

I grabbed the phone, dialed the number of Barbara Davis in Anaheim, California. I didn't know what I was going to say. Ring ring. A tiny ancient voice picked up, a voice so clotted with years I could barely hear the words. In the background, a dog was barking. "Shut up, Juno," the ancient woman said.

"Are you Barb Davis?" I asked.

"I'm Barb-ar-a," she croaked. "Who're you?"

"I'm . . . I'm . . ." a sudden stutter. I couldn't say my name. And this, I knew, beyond a shadow of a doubt, was not the Barbara I'd spent so many months talking to.

"Who is this?" the old lady, the total stranger barked.

"I'm . . ." I said.

"Who is this?" she screeched again.

I hung up then, fast. Good question. Who am I?

You might want to know why I didn't just throw in the towel. Why would I first be compelled to have a bizarre relationship with a telephone-voice, and then, when it didn't pan out, to actually try to unravel it? You might want to know why I didn't just say, *Okay, the world is full of loonies,* and then walk away. Frankly, I want to know that too.

As a superhero, I am sworn to serve. I have no choice really. This need to save people is so strange, because it comes from such a warped place inside me: On the one hand, I think I'm powerful enough to really make a difference; it's sheer disgusting narcissism. On the other hand, I feel so powerless, so much like the people I am trying to help, that I blur the line between me and them.

And then there was Stacie herself. Stacie, whoever she was, had become a friend and a reflection, a conduit to the pieces of my own past, pieces I was aware of but had not resolved. There are things that happen in your own life that you'll never resolve; you just keep shaping and reshaping them, like a sculptor. If I let Stacie go, I was letting go of a chance to get close to my own trauma. That makes sense, doesn't it? But it was still more than that. Part of it was just sheer raw neurological compulsion. Present me with a puzzle and I'll solve it or die trying. I hate unknowns, maybes, and this, this was the mother of all maybes.

I called the police back. I said, "I know you can't tell me about criminal records, but can you tell me anything? Was there a rape of a fourteen-year-old girl, by a youth minister?"

"Rosie," the policewoman said. "I have lived here my whole life. No, there was not."

"Can you tell me anything? At all?" I begged.

She paused for a while. "Give me the number you have been calling," she said. I did. "Okay, I can tell you this, that number is registered to a Melissa Star. She is thirty-eight."

Melissa Star? Sounded like a stripper. I needed more. "That's it, nothing else? Please." I sounded pathetic.

"Rosie, I can't . . . well, let's just say we are familiar with that address here at the station. That's all I am going to say."

Well, that was vague enough to drive me out of my mind. "Thank you," I said, and hung up.

Now I was officially mad. I was pissed off. No con artist idiot was gonna take advantage of me and get away with it. I was gonna confront her. I stared at my television set: *Unsolved Mysteries* played silently muted, how appropriate. I picked up the phone and dialed the number I now knew by heart.

A strange voice answered.

"Melissa," I said, and I felt pure rage. I was standing, pacing, all puffed up like a big frog.

"Yeah," the voice answered.

"This is Rosie," I said, and then paused, giving her a minute to absorb the shock, that she'd been caught, that I'd nailed her real name.

"Huh?" she said, kind of flat, and then she said, weirder than weird, "I've been making cookies."

This was not the response I expected. I expected a sharp intake of breath, maybe even panic, profuse apologies, a hang-up, but not a cookie report.

"Oh," I said. "What kind?"

"Nutter Butter," she said.

What the hell is going on here? I thought. No one *makes* Nutter Butters. You have to buy them.

"The jig is up," I said. "Why don't you tell me what it is you've been doing with me all these months."

"Who is this?" she asked, confused, like she was just waking up from a nap.

"Rosie O'Donnell," I spit out, with authority, like Cagney or Lacey.

"From TV?" she said.

"Yeah," I said. "From TV."

There was silence on the line and then she said, "Who is this, Mindy? Dawn?"

Spingle. Something clicked. I don't know what, but something clicked. Her confusion. All these names. The flatness of her voice. It was a little like speaking to a sleepwalker, and my anger morphed into compassion. This woman had something seriously wrong with her. She was not caught, not acting, not lying. She honestly did not believe it was me, she had no idea what I was talking about. She did not hang up on me, she did not try to wiggle her way out. She just stayed on the line and waited for my reply. Was I Mindy or Dawn?

I asked Melissa if she saw a shrink. She told me yeah, she did, and then rattled off the number without much concern.

"Do you mind if I call her?" I asked.

"It's your life," she said and then she hung up.

So I called her shrink. It was late, almost eleven in Miami, but earlier in Oregon. I assumed it was an office number, that I would leave a message. It wasn't. A woman answered.

"Is this Tina Lano?" I asked.

"Yes."

"Do you treat a woman named Melissa Star?" I asked calmly.

"Who is this?" A good question, I thought. Maybe she really was a shrink. I thought for a moment it was Melissa/Barb, continuing the con. I told her my name. She had never heard of me. I told her I had a talk show, like Oprah's, only funny and without as much meaning. She said she did not watch TV. I gave her the details of my relationship with Stacie, with Barb, with Melissa. She asked me to hold on, she needed to get a pen. She took notes as I went over the whole saga. When I was done she asked me for my phone number. She told me she wanted to verify what I had told her, and she would get back to me.

"Is she a multiple?" I asked, hoping for something, a tiny crumb even.

"I will call you tomorrow," she said, evenly, like a shrink.

*　　*　　*

I knew I was right. I really knew it. There is no way to explain knowing, you just do. If you are one who gets the knowing nod from the great beyond, you understand. If you never have, just believe, that some people do know, even before they are told. I knew. I called Melissa back.

"Listen, this is Rosie again. Hey, I understand. I am going to call you tomorrow after I talk with Tina. It is all going to be okay."

She hung up on me again.

It was very late then. I needed sleep. I fingered the smooth stones on my nightstand, good-luck charms. I actually believe in charms, in stars, in serendipity. Nothing happens by chance. This woman reached out to me, and for some odd reason, I reached back. We get hundreds of calls every month from birth mothers; this was the only one I returned personally. This was the one that spoke to me. She knocked on the door, and I opened it. Nothing happens by chance.

I fell down then, into a deep, deep sleep.

Tina Lano called the next day. She had never heard of me, but her son had. Turns out he regularly attends a cystic fibrosis ski event I host every year. He had a photo with me on his desk at work. He listened to his mother's story and said, "Yes, Mom, that's her. I bet she would do that." Tina's son verified me, and Melissa had given Tina the okay, so that next day I got the whole story.

"She does have multiple personality disorder," said Tina. "And her alters are named Stacie and Barb, and Doug, and then there's also a Nancy and a Kate and several others. A few months ago Melissa lost her job, she's been seriously depressed, and that's caused the personalities to resurface again."

"What can I do to help?" I said. "Can I give money, set up a trust?"

I heard my own voice. It had an impulsive sound to it.

"Why would you want to give money," Tina asked, "to a person you don't even know?"

Suddenly I felt like I was Tina's patient.

I shrugged, on the phone, not the most effective way of communicating.

"Sometimes," I said, "oftentimes, I feel like I have to help the whole world. Why, why *is* that?" I said.

"It's narcissism," Tina said. I liked this lady. She laid it straight out. "You think you're powerful enough to change things, and it keeps you, I'm sure, from having to really work on yourself."

"Whatever," I said. Defeated at being pegged so easily.

"Dissociative identity disorder," said Tina, "is the result of severe childhood trauma. Melissa has endured things that are so far out of the ordinary, she could only cope with them by splitting into separate selves." She then listed a condensed version of horrors, so grotesque I asked her to stop.

"Enough!" I said. "Please, how can I help her?"

Melissa's horrors. My own head was swimming. I went outside then, where it was hot. As hell. Tina had told me Melissa had watched her own cousin being burned almost to death by an aunt. Hot. As hell. Sometimes you get to the point where the whole world stops making sense. Where the violence overwhelms. Where your own history pushes up against someone else's. I knew my own history, but there are different ways of knowing; sometimes you get to a deeper level. I realized that no amount of therapy, giving away of money, or involvement with other wounded travelers would take away my own damage. I knew I had avoided fully experiencing my own past by living in other people's.

I remember reading once in some magazine article that doctors took pictures of trauma survivors' brains and compared them to normal brains, and the traumatized brains were different. The point of that story is that trauma gets stamped into the brain's gray mush—the doctors in the article called it a trauma tattoo—and that seems like a good description for the way bad things get chiseled right into your head so no matter how hard you shake your head, they won't go away.

Nothing happens by chance.

CHAPTER 24

Does the trauma tattoo look the same on every brain? I wonder, do all swamp people have a big Gothic double T in black ink stamped on the cerebellum? Were Melissa/Stacie and I all marked?

Tattoos are addictive. I have two. One on my right ankle, one on my left arm. Together they are a culmination of seven trips to tattoo parlors. I have made myself what I never thought I would, a tattooed person.

When I was a kid, someone convinced me bad guys were easy to spot. There were things to look for, dirty hair, black T-shirts, jiggly eyes, and tattoos. A tattoo said something. It said, *I am dangerous, look out for me, beware.* The person who told me this was a bad guy. He had clean hair, bright clothes, calm eyes, and no tattoos. He wore a costume of kindness over an essence of crud.

Most people who get tattoos are marking a moment, a subtle shift in sensibility, a transition from one mind-set to another. My first tattoo was just that. I was lost. A tornado of emotions picked me up, spun me around, and dropped me in a foreign land. I was scared and scarred, weak and worried. I made it out, somehow. I found a metaphorical machete and chopped at the dark ugliness before me in search of a life light I knew existed. I arrived safe, but forever changed. On my first day of freedom, I got a tattoo.

I drove down the boulevard and stopped in front of a run-down storefront. TATTOO glared out at me in red neon. I went inside. I heard "Lemme know if you have any questions" called out from the back as I looked at the tattoos on display. There were so many to chose from: Chinese symbols, tigers, dragons, psychotic clowns, and beer-bellied baby angels all on display, laminated and hung haphazardly on every surface. A big burly biker man came out from the back, smiled, and said, "I can draw whatever you want. Just ask." He then went about cleaning his station.

A tattoo parlor is a lot like a dentist's office. Both have reclining chairs so you can relax while you are getting done. The artist, like a dentist, has a tool, a gun, almost a drill. In fact, the noise it makes is very similar to that of a dentist's drill, only with a lot more bass. There are tons of tiny pinkie-sized plastic cups to hold the ink. You would be amazed at how little ink is used. Just a few Barbie coffee mugs full of rainbow goop.

After an hour we had our design, a cross with a heart and a rose. He sketched it on tracing paper and put it through a ditto machine, which turned it into a press-on outline. He pressed it on the inside of my right ankle, barely noticeable. I wanted a tattoo but didn't know if I was brave enough to wear one. I played it safe, just two and a half inches long, on my rarely seen inner leg. I could, and would, cover it with a sock.

I left an hour after I went in, a changed person. Only eighty dollars for personal freedom, for reclaiming a body that had betrayed me, for defining myself. I was a person with a tattoo. And if anyone thought that made me a bad guy, they were wrong. One day they would wake up. I understood, they, too, had been misled. I knew, I used to be one of them.

So in the midst of my Melissa Madness, I decide to get my tiny tattoo turned into a rather huge work of art. It had been through many incarnations since that first hidden cross a decade before. It had become a thin band of roses and then a whole bouquet of flowers. It was hand drawn and uneven, a hodgepodge. I wanted a new one, one that suited the me I was now, the me I had become. I wanted grit, reality 101.

Anil Gupta, the tattoo artist, asked me what I

wanted. I told him, "Get rid of the flowers, give me grit and gears. Make my skin looked ripped, revealing gears underneath like a machine, with some vines growing through the chaos in defiance." Okay, he said. That's it. Okay.

It was eight o'clock when I looked up. We had been working for six hours straight. I sat in stoic silence, as the gun buzzed and my skin burned. I thought of Stacie and Melissa. I wondered where they were, if they felt safe. What was it we were supposed to learn from each other? I knew, deep inside, I could not save them.

My leg was throbbing in a way I love, pleasure pain, sought-out suffering. It hurt and it didn't. I was riding the pain like a wave when the doorbell rang. It was Richie; I recognized him right away from Anil's Web site. Richie is a walking canvas of Anil's best work, a living, breathing piece of art. I called out to him, asking him to come into the back room where I was sitting. I don't know why I asked him in, but I did. He came in laughing. Richie is shy and smiling, distracted and deliberate. He has a frenetic energy most adults dismiss as childish. I found him captivating.

Tattoo parlors are the ultimate equalizers. A spiritual melting pot. Richie the chemist and Vietnam vet, me the talk show host and mom, and Anil, the artist and husband. There are few places the three of us would ever meet. Our circles in the outside world would not intersect. But here in the tattoo parlor, we were together, sharing this moment, burning into my soul a memory, as the ink stained my skin.

I asked to see Richie's tattoos. He showed his right leg first, King Tut in bold gold. Huge and stunning. A monkey eating a pickle was next, on his left arm, all magic and serenity. I asked what he was working on now, and Richie hesitated. He fidgeted with his belt buckle and then tried to change the subject. I pushed. He dropped his pants. Down four inches below his tighty whiteys was a large new piece. A replica of the Vietnam Veterans Memorial, half done, on his left thigh. Three soldiers walking back from battle, tired and worn, delicately etched, with shadows and shading. Even unfinished, it was astounding.

Richie stayed for the rest of my session; nearly two hours more. We talked about movies and Scrabble, computers and comedy. He listens intently, holding your eyes. He is authentic, without airs, he is the real deal, this Richie.

I saw him catch sight of my scar. The new one that lives on my left wrist. The one that looks like I tried to end it all. He saw it and looked away, embarrassed, I thought, by what he was thinking. As if he had seen me naked, and wished he hadn't. I waited for his eyes to once again reach mine. They did. "Did you want to ask me anything, Richie?" He answered no, shaking his head in confirmation. Then no again.

I waited. After twenty minutes of silence he

asked me, quickly, "What happened to your wrist, Rosie?" He did not look at me when he asked. Sensing his dread, I told him, as fast as I could, about my surgery. I let him know, without saying it, no. No I had not deliberately hurt myself. It was an accident, not an incident. Silence again.

His compassion was empathy, no doubt. He knew the places on his body that held eternal exit signs. The thought had crossed his mind once or twice. Exit.

I got it all, this unspoken conversation. Richie's brain, I am sure, has a Gothic double T, same as mine.

"Well, Rosie," he said, "what doesn't kill you makes you stronger. Right, Rosie? Right?" His eyes were pleading, he needed convincing. We both did.

"Yes, Richie, that's true. What doesn't kill you makes you stronger."

Some days I believe it.

For the rest of my session I told Richie and Anil about me and Stacie. They listened without judgment as I told it, for the first time, without shame.

CHAPTER 25

At this point, my show runs smoothly. Six years ago, at the beginning, I had my hands in everything, but now there is no need. My staff is excellent; they know what to do. They are quite competent. We also have college interns, and I swear, I have never had sex with any of them.

I have an unusual work space. I am told it looks a little like a pediatrician's office. It's fun, because I need it to be fun. If I could, I would live in Toon Town, with splashes of orange-yellow and goblin-green, bright blue and really red red. When we first moved in, the space was dreary. It was office-gray with ugly partitions every few feet. I hated it. We fixed it. Now, when you come to our office, you fall into a kaleido-scope of colors, red chairs with heart-shaped backs, walls in primary yellows, tiny trolls with spigots of hair in corners. There are small sur-prises everywhere.

My show was a success from day one. Fate, destiny, or pure luck? Who knows? In any case, the suits were very pleased. They were making tons of dough. A few days after I learned who the "real" Barb and Stacie Davis were, a few days after I spoke with Melissa and Tina, Jim, my personal suit, asked me for a meeting. "Just us," he said.

We met in my office. He offered me an insane amount of money if I agreed to renew my contract for another two years. It was more money than a human being could ever spend in one lifetime.

I fiddled with a pen. I shrugged my shoulders. Fame is more than money. I thought of Madonna. Being friends with her gave me an insider's view of celebrity, at a time when I was chasing it. Strangers stopped her in the street, often crying, overwhelmed by her image, shocked by her presence. People commented on her as if she could not hear them. "Hey Madonna, your hair looks better blond"—as if anyone asked.

Fame is weird. It affects everything and everyone it touches. When do you have enough? When do you say, *No more for me, thanks?* When do you realize the race is over, and it's time to take off your sneakers?

I was ready. I was sure. It would be very movie-of-the-week-ish if I attributed this solely to my relationship with Melissa/Stacie. No, it wasn't just that, but it did have some effect. So did other things, like being thirty-nine and realizing I'd outlived my own mother, wanting more time for friends and family, seeing how the TV me and the "real me" were growing farther and farther apart.

"So," said Jim, "what about the offer?"

"It's not about the money, Jim," I said. "I have enough money. . . . It's been an amazing thing, this show, in so many ways, but . . ."

Jim said, "With an offer like this, Rosie, why are you even pausing? You will never see this kind of money again. Ever again."

I said, "Jim, if you have fifty million dollars, and you think you need fifty million more, you have lost your mind." I am convinced of that. Anil, my tattoo artist, once told me, "There is always enough for need, but never enough for greed."

Jim looked at me, confused.

"Listen," I said. "It's about wanting to be a more authentic person, not just the part of myself I show on TV. There is more to me, more to my life, to being an artist, to being alive, than doing this show. I have done it. I feel finished."

"Hey, whatever you want to do or say, we at Telepictures would stand behind you 100 percent, no matter what it was."

That was sweet, I thought. I could spend an hour a day ranting about the perils of gun ownership, the need for Head Start, the plight of foster children, without having to worry about the front office. Tempting.

"Thanks, Jim. It is something bigger and I doubt I can fully explain it," I said. "On my show I'm always in this weird position. I'm supposed to reveal just enough about me so that people feel close to me, but I can't really be . . . me."

"Rosie, what are you, Pinocchio, the Velveteen Rabbit?" Jim said. "You don't see it, but you are so *you* on your show."

"No," I said. "I am not."

"Listen, Rosie," he said, almost meekly, "we can work out the details, shoot in Miami . . . whatever it takes."

I stayed quiet.

"Think it over," he said and left. I let him have the last word. Men like that.

• • •

Ever since I was a kid, I have loved to read. My favorite books were Nancy Drew, Hardy Boys, Judy Blume. I read my first novel when I was in the seventh grade, and from then on I was hooked. I used to read on hot summer days, in the dead of winter, in the dark, the wafer circle of a flashlight illuminating the page, my sister Maureen asleep in her bed beside mine. Even as a very small child, words on a page drew me. In first grade the teacher taught us how to read. I thought I would

never learn. Letters on the blackboard were separated by dashes, like C-A-T, or D-A-D, and she'd
have us sound them out. I hated those dashes
breaking up the letters, and I remember struggling so hard to bring it all together. D-O-G.
Under the too-bright lights of our first-grade
classroom I said, "DDDDOOOOOGGGGGGG,"
and, *baboom*, a flash in my brain. Dog, dog! I did
it! It all came together; the dashes went away.
With the word *dog*, the world had meaning, the
broken bits were gone, and words linked up to
tell a tale.

I decided to buy Melissa and company a computer so we could e-mail. I got her an account on
AOL, but it turned out she had no phone line; it
had been disconnected. I got her a phone line,
but it turned out she couldn't sign on. So—well,
I actually sent a tech team out there to Oregon to
hook her up. At one point she called me, from
the phone line I'd bought her, and asked, "How
much is this costing you, Rosie? You have done
enough. I don't want you spending money on
us." I said, totally lying, "Don't worry, Melissa, it's
my old, used computer, it didn't cost me a cent."

"This computer is brand-new, it is still in the
box," Melissa said.

Busted. So I 'fessed up, and she got mad. I didn't
know if she would keep the computer or send it
back. I half expected to see the PowerBook on
my front step a few days later.

*   *   *

141

But that's not what happened. We started in on an e-mail correspondence. The written word. I enjoyed that in some ways more than the phone, seeing my sentences pop up there on the screen. It was very, very strange to be corresponding with a multiple. I followed Tina's advice and wrote to Melissa only, but Melissa would answer me in different alters, depending on the day. To tell you the truth, I found that tremendously exciting, and totally addictive. I began to think of myself almost as, well, almost as a shrink, or my own movie version of a shrink doing "deep" work and patting myself on the back for my ability to engage this woman. (I make myself sick.) Where in this impulse is there generosity, if at all? I don't know the answer. Giving has a dark side, a selfish side. This much I can say for sure.

In all our e-mails, Stacie did not once appear. I found myself missing her during the day. I knew she wasn't real but she was real, to me. One day I watched a skinny eight-year-old girl with dirty-blond hair play with an old dog on the sidewalk. That's what Stacie looked like as a kid, I found myself thinking. Stacie, who didn't really exist.

Another day I saw a plane dragging a banner in the blue, and the banner read R.S.V.P. A.S.A.P. It was an ad for a gay cruise line. Carolyn was walking with me and she said, "Now don't make that into anything, Ro." I shrugged. Spingle. Sometimes, the world is so full of signs, hints, splashes of light to lead your way.

I e-mailed with Melissa. We "instant messaged" each other:

— hello
— Kate wrote me
— my arms are burned
— I did two shows today
— sorry she wrote you, was it mean
— I can take it
— you work too much
— do they hurt
— not so much, I am used to it

But at no point did the girl I'd come to love emerge. I missed her, my little Stacie. I ending up meeting the others.

CHAPTER 26

E-mails. They started off slow, then came fast and furious. Melissa's different alters, except for Stacie, started to emerge with more and more speed. When I turned on my computer, I wasn't sure which voice would greet me. All the voices were different, some pristine and mannered—"Good morning, Rosie, how are you?"—the grammar impeccable, all Grand Dame. Other voices were rough, angry, even almost illiterate. My head swam.

Hold on, here we go.

Subj: hi
To: STARGAL
From: RO3456
HEY . . .
DID YOU FIGURE OUT HOW TO USE THE COMPUTER I SENT YOU YET? LEMME KNOW BY SENDING ME A NOTE BACK. I HOPE YOU

LIKE THE COMPUTER. IT'S THE SAME ONE I
USE.
LOVE
ROSIE

Subj: hey
To: STARGAL
From: RO3456
You haven't written me back. . . .
Wasssuppppp?
How is it going?
Love
Rosie

Subj: powerbook
To: STARGAL
From: RO3456
A lot of people like IBM, but I have always been a
Mac person. It's easy, just point and click. If you are
having trouble, you can call me and I will try to talk
you through getting on-line. Although if you're not
on-line, you're not reading this now. Whatever.
Love
Rosie

To: STARGAL
From: RO3456
Hey you, the mail you are sending me is empty. You
have to type first and then hit send now. Let me
know if you need help with it.
Okay.

Write back soon.
Love
Rosie

Now I'd like to say that the "Love Rosie" strikes me as odd. First off, I rarely use that name. Looking back, my signing "love" to a person I did not know seems sort of sad.

It took Melissa two weeks to reply. I had almost given up on her when I heard those three little words I love so . . . "you've got mail!"

Subj: WHO KNOWS
To: RO3456
From: STARGAL
I'm evaluating things at the present moment, I don't
really know what has been going on today or at all.
I'm sorry that Stacie and Barb and everyone has
been bothering you for so long. I cannot keep them
under wraps but I will try. Haven't been myself at
all today.
Maybe tomorrow will be a better day. This sucks.
It's dark out!
Melissa

To: STARGAL
From: RO3456
Mel,
Stacie never bothered me. She was, is my friend. I
know what it's like not to be yourself, and to feel
afraid of the dark. I hate to go out at night, fear I

147

guess. I still think there are boogie men in the bushes. When you have a crappy childhood, it affects everything in your adult life, as I am sure you know.

Lemme know how you are feeling.

I miss Stacie, I think about her a lot.

Love

Rosie

To: RO3456

From: STARGAL

Dear Rosie,

Somebody must have slept, that's good, I feel better. Today will be a good day because I feel a lot better now that somebody slept. It's almost like my body gives out and it figures out that we have to sleep and we do.

I think I am going to try to clean the house again. It's such a mess in here. My legs are totally numb. Maybe I can find the counter and the table. I can't believe I can't get this done.

Mel (Nancy)

To: RO3456

From: STARGAL

Rosie,

You're gonna wish you would never have sent this computer to us. I'm finding little notes all over the place and everyone wants to know how to do this. Kate is a little pissed about it. Have you met Kate? Sometimes she hurts people; she burns us. I wrote computer instructions down but I don't know if anyone has it figured out. There are some that don't even know who you are. I hate to admit it but I didn't always watch your show. It comes on at 4 P.M. and that was normally the time I was getting home from work. Now that I have all the time in the world I normally watch it. I think it's a good show. I can't wait to see tomorrow's. Maybe when I give everyone permission to listen in they will see who you are. And then get back with you if they can figure this computer out. My mind is getting clearer now thanks for listening. We are always open for suggestions.

Thanks

Nancy

Nancy, it turned out, was the writer of the group. She and I would become very close.

CHAPTER 27

In the days of vaudeville, the tap dancer was always ready, waiting in the wings. If a new act wasn't going over well, if one of the comics was having an off night, if the crowd was getting impatient, the emcee would send out the tapper. A distraction, something familiar, a way to calm the chaos.

I am going to tap dance for you now, because I know it's getting weird. The story seems so insane, unbelievable, almost scary. I feel you need a break.

George Burns.

I never met him, but I did speak to him on the phone. He had a standing date to headline Caesars Palace in Las Vegas on his one hundredth birthday—January 20, 1996. He lived to see one hundred but was not well enough to perform on that date. They asked me to fill in for him. It is not possible to "fill in" for George Burns, not on his hundredth birthday, not ever, but I said I would do my best, if they could not find anyone more appropriate. They didn't. So I did. A weekend gig, two shows a night, the main room. I had worked Caesars Palace before, both as an opening act and as a headliner.

The first time, I opened for David Copperfield. He is a magician, an illusionist, a guy who can make things disappear. Night one, I sucked. I did my act, one I had honed for many years on the road, one that worked, at least somewhat, every night I had done it, for more than a decade. I was booked to do twenty minutes. I did them, without one laugh. I was sure I would be fired. I spent the rest of the night in a panic, waiting for the word to pack my bags. David finished, I went back to my room, no one said anything. That was that.

The next night I pulled out all the stops. I was in comic overdrive. I killed. I slayed them, I left them screaming for more. Yes! This is what I knew I could do. Such relief. I was in my dressing room, riding the adrenaline, when I heard the knock on my door.

Someone thanking me, I thought, telling me how good I was, how great I did. I opened the door, smiling. A large man I had not met before stood in front of me in a suit. He was not smiling.

"Miss O'Donnell, are you aware of what you did tonight?" he asked.

I smirked, kind of embarrassed. I did really well, I knew it, but I wasn't going to say it. I just nodded.

"You did twenty-four minutes. You were contracted to do twenty minutes. Do you have any idea how much this hotel makes on two thousand people in four minutes? Approximately two hundred thousand dollars. When you are ready to write a check for that amount to this hotel, then you can do an extra four minutes. Do I make myself clear?"

I was stunned. I was shocked.

"But they laughed, a lot . . . remember last night . . . they didn't laugh at all . . . I was funny tonight . . . did you see it?"

"Yeah, I saw it. All twenty-four minutes. You were supposed to do twenty. Tomorrow, do twenty, kid. And last night was a convention, from Japan. Nobody spoke English. They came to see the magic." And with that he left.

The next night I did exactly twenty minutes. I went out and bought a digital stopwatch with a beeping alarm. I set it for nineteen minutes, thirty seconds. When it beeped, I stopped, mid-joke, and thanked the crowd, and was off the stage with ten seconds to spare. My suited friend was waiting for me in the wings. He looked at his watch, winked, and said, "Thatta girl."

So I did my first night on the stage where George Burns should have been. The crowd was sweet, their love for him evident as they sang happy birthday in unison. The next morning I was in my room when the phone rang.

"George Burns calling for Miss O'Donnell," a young man said. My heart started beating, loudly. I told the man it was me and he asked me to hold on. I stood up. When I get really excited I have to stand up. I waited, then I heard it, his voice, so recognizable, so familiar it made me smile.

"Rosie . . . Rosie, how are you doing, sweetheart?"

"Fine sir, thank you. It is wonderful of you to call, we all missed you last night."

"A full house?"

"Yes sir, sold out, all of them expecting to see you. I was no substitute."

"I hear you did fine. . . . Listen, Rosie, do you know what the doorman at the sperm bank says when people leave?"

"No sir."

"Thank you for coming."

I laughed, amazed that this legendary man, sickly and one hundred years old, was telling me jokes, a private show, one of his last, it turned out.

"You are Irish, right, honey? Did you hear about the Irish woman who saved all her money and decided to take a milk bath . . . she called

154

the milkman and asked how many gallons of milk she would need to fill up her bathtub. And the milkman said, "About twenty gallons. Would . . . would you like it pasteurized?"

She said, "No, just past my titties."

My God, I laughed, I didn't see that one coming. We talked for a few minutes, about my new television show. How I wanted to capture the spirit of Merv Griffin, how I would love to have him as a guest.

"That would be lovely, sweetheart, but I think I am going to go see Gracie soon."

I said good-bye. He died three weeks later.

As I hung up the phone, I ached for my mother. I wanted her to share this all with me. Las Vegas. George Burns. My son.

CHAPTER 28

Parker. The boy I got was most definitely a girl, they assured me. There was no question. They did a sonogram; I was having a girl. I was ready for a girl, I had nieces, I was a girl, girls I knew. Boys were a mystery. I knew nothing of boys, and what I knew of men was no enticement to boy-raising.

I was on the kitchen floor cleaning out the fridge when the phone rang. After two hours of labor, out he came, tiny and perfect and male. The social worker, knowing I was ready for a girl, had that tone of voice that raises neck hairs, happy but wanting. Something was wrong. I was in a panic . . . did the birth mother change her mind? My heart was pounding, I had to fight to stay in my body. "Is there a problem? What's the problem?"

"No problem," she said. "You have a healthy son."

She must have said more, but I didn't hear it. Son? A boy. I had a boy. How could that be? I was fairly certain I was supposed to have a girl. Not because of any sonogram but because I thought God wanted me to have a girl. I had dead-mother stuff to work out, surely my life lessons would be learned through my daughter. A boy, what would I do with a boy? There must have been a pause, because the social worker asked, "Are you okay? Any questions?"

"Yeah," I said, "when is he coming home?"

He spent the night of his birth in the hospital; I spent mine wide-awake, unable to sleep for even a moment. I wished someone would arrive with an epidural, Valium, Xanax, something. No such luck. Just me and the television. At 3 A.M. I found an amazing documentary on cable. It was produced and narrated by Jane Goodall, a woman who has spent her life in search of the meaning in monkeys, the good in us all. I was captivated.

A family of chimps, some of whom had polio, were struggling to survive in a land where living wasn't easy. Chimps were poached daily, killed for their hands or sold to zoos. As if that weren't enough, these chimps were fighting among themselves. It was crisis central. Babies were born and lost, mothers grieved. It was a soap opera, Pine Valley of the primates. They had the matriarch (à la Ruth Martin), the lovingly steady leading lady, going gray trying to keep her dignity while being tortured by her adolescent son (à la Tad). The "Tad" chimp was trouble. He loved his mother but was the last of her many children; by the time he was born, she was already too old to parent. When he became a teenage chimp, he was rowdy and overtly mean to everyone. The mom tried to control him; you could see her screaming eyes, pleading, begging, *Tad, behave, you are a good boy, please.* . . .

It was too late; this monkey/boy was out of control. He killed his sister's infant son in a jealous rage. The bereft sister carried her baby's lifeless body for weeks. Even dead, Tad still attacked the boy. Ruth Martin finally gave up. As the family made their way through the jungle in search of a new home, she lay down on the river's edge and died. The tribe was in turmoil. Where to go? What to do? Who would be their leader? In desperation they looked to Tad. He was nowhere to be found. After stroking his dead mother's head, trying to lift her lifeless body from the mud, after howling for hours, Tad climbed a tree directly above his mom's body, and there he stayed. He would not eat or drink, he only cried. It was excruciating to watch, impossible to turn away from. The filmmakers, so touched by his grief, so consumed with his sorrow, did what documentary filmmakers never do—they intervened. They climbed up to him, offering food and water. The chimp was unmoved. He ignored their gifts. Ten days later, he was dead. The film was over, the sun was rising. I got up and washed the tears from my face, and waited the four long hours till my son arrived.

I paced the floors and watched for the blue Volvo station wagon that held my son. The moment I knew would completely alter my life. I thought I was prepared; no one ever is. The doorbell rang. I opened the door and saw a tiny yellow blanket with slick matted black hair sticking straight up. I reached for him, as he did me. When he was in my arms, he opened his eyes. Black-blue pools of steel staring right into me. *Hi, Mama,* I heard inside. *Here we go.*

I told him that night, as he took his midnight feeding, of my jungle friends. Of a baby chimp who loved his mother so, it ended up killing them both. How love is not enough, but when given and received with grace, dignity, and respect, anything is possible.

My baby boy is now a first-grader. I am a fun but strict mom. When he complains, as he does often, I think about that baby chimp. Nothing happens by chance. I have a son—in fact I now have two. I have learned not to second-guess God. Things are not always as they seem. There are treasures right beneath our eyes. This boy of mine has brought me to a new level of loving, beyond the beyond. A place I had dreamed of, but never knew was real.

Hi Mama, here we go.

CHAPTER 29

To: STARGAL
From: RO3456
Hey Nancy
I hope all of you do write me. I think it would be
amazing to know all the parts of you. Barb and
Stacie are both kind and sensitive and smart. I liked
talking to them.
I am putting the kiddies to bed and I am going to
watch celeb millionaire. I guess you getting the
computer didn't cause major problems within.
That's good. I am hoping Kate won't be mad. No, I
have not met her. Who knows, she just might like
me. You don't have to say sorry for writing me. I
like it. Any luck cleaning the house? I have a little
OCD, I let it get messy then go on a binge . . .
organizing every little thing. I am off to bed.
Love, Rosie

To: RO3456
From: STARGAL
Rosie,

No, I didn't get the house cleaned but I did get the water run in the sink. I have no idea where the day went but I know Stacie was here anyway, she said she didn't have a clue about this computer and wouldn't touch it. Maybe I can change our minds tonight. I think she's mad she can't talk to you. She's acting like a spoiled brat. Teenagers anyway. I don't know what Tina has told you about Kate but she is into pretty sick stuff. I've been trying to figure that one out for a long time and it's totally blocked. I can tell you this much. When we were about six or seven years old we watched our aunt burn our cousin, I can remember him screaming. She burned him from his neck down to his toes. I can still hear him sometimes, that's probably what everybody has nightmares about and probably why we scream. I don't know everything Tina told you and that's kind of scary. She probably didn't tell you much, otherwise you wouldn't even want to know us. I know that much. I think we scare all the therapists away, everyone but Tina. Well here I go again just on and on and on about nothing. I'll let you go. Bye for now.

Mel (Nancy)

To: STARGAL
From: RO3456
Nancy,

Tina told me you have DID and that you had been very abused as a kid. I am sorry about all that. Did your cousin die? Who else saw it? Did she get arrested? I bet not. Seems like you can do anything to a kid and get away with it.

All I know about Kate is Tina said she is the one who is sometimes mean, and causes physical harm to your body. Everyone has anger and I guess having one person hold it all makes sense. Maybe Kate can talk to me, she won't be so mad and/or scared. Mostly anger is about feeling hurt by someone and wanting to hurt back. I get it.

I would love to hear about your childhood. All and anything you want to share. I got you this computer so we could get to know each other better.

Sometimes at work it's hard for me, cause there are so many people around. This summer, when I was talking to Stacie and Barb, it was easier, cause I wasn't working.

So don't worry about me being grossed out. I know it is hard to talk about. I am hoping writing it will be easier. Writing is sometimes truer than talk.

I am not going anywhere.

Love Rosie

CHAPTER 30

Kick ball-change, kick ball-change, shuffle step, shuffle step.

Some things about my dad:

He likes rocky road ice cream and historical novels.
He listens to the Clancy Brothers and Neil Diamond.
He is one of eight children.
He was not loved enough.

He used to go to the bank on Saturday morning. Sometimes I went with him. He was good at one-on-one, my dad. All five of us at once would send him over the edge.

It was just me and him alone in the car. I sitting in the front seat, without a seat belt. It was 1971; I was nine. We went inside the bank, although I asked to do the drive-through, because I loved the vacuum tube roller thing that magically sucked your money away. Very Jetsons.

We waited in line, a maze of velvet ropes. My dad signed his check, and I got a lollipop. We were back in the car, in the parking lot, my dad was counting his cash, his weekly salary from Grumman, where he designed cameras, spy satellites. "You know, doll, right now, those Russians can read our license plate." His common refrain, which caused me, years later, to run screaming into therapy: "They are watching us! They are watching us!"

"Let's go, Dad," I said, anxious to get home with some of my lolly left, so I could show off to my sibs.

"We have to go back in, looks like they made a mistake, dolly."

My dad calls me dolly, even now, without thinking. The story goes that I was a new baby with two older sibs who were just learning to speak. *Roseann* was the name I got, one they could not say. "She looks like a dolly," my three-year-old brother Eddie said. And it stuck. Dolly it was, until I made them stop. My dad can't seem to help himself.

So we walk back into the bank, my tiny hand in his, trying to keep up with his long-legged grown-up gait. He cuts the line and goes back to the same cashier he had minutes earlier, a woman who lives somewhere in our neighborhood. I have seen her before. She looks like everyone's mom, only older. I can't hear what they are talking about; they both smile, she turns a little red, then we are back in the car.

"How much money was it, Dad?"

"Sixty dollars."

"Wow, good thing you caught it, that's a lot of money," I said.

"It's not about the money, doll."

I didn't say anything. I knew he was lying, sixty bucks was a bundle.

"When that woman checked out after her shift, her tray would have been short."

"No, Dad! Duh! She would just have *more* money then she should have. Not less."

"No, she would have been sixty dollars short, doll. She gave me too much money."

It took a moment. Too much money? Extra cash? Free dough? We could have just driven away a little bit richer!

"Why did you give it back?" I asked.

"Because it is the right thing to do, doll."

And that was that.

For all he was not able to do, there were still things he did. He set my moral compass, my dad. There is right and wrong. Only two choices, you choose.

CHAPTER 31

To: RO3456
From: STARGAL
Hey Rosie,
No, my cousin didn't die. Not then anyway. He
killed himself, I think he was like thirty-two years
old it was about four or five years ago. He had four
kids and a wife. He overdosed on his dad's
birthday. That was his present I guess. His mom
never got in trouble. We were so scared all the time.
This sounds so crazy doesn't it?
Melissa (Nancy)

To: RO3456
From: STARGAL
Hey whoever you are go and see the blood it's cool
and the baby will be full of it don't forget about the
blood don't talk about the aunt again we are next to
die everyone of us and she will be close she will
laugh at us she will be close

169

To: STARGAL

From: RO3456

KATE,

HI. MY NAME IS ROSIE O'DONNELL. I AM
FRIENDS WITH NANCY AND STACIE AND BARB
AND MELISSA. THANKS FOR WRITING TO ME.
I AM NOT AFRAID OF YOUR AUNT, AND NO
ONE IS GOING TO DIE. WE ARE ALL GROWN
UP NOW AND NO ONE CAN HURT US.
I WOULD LIKE TO GET TO KNOW YOU, KATE.
SO, IF YOU WANT, WRITE ME BACK. EVEN IF
IT'S ABOUT BLOOD, THAT'S OKAY.
THERE IS NOTHING YOU CAN SAY THAT WILL
MAKE ME MAD, BECAUSE I UNDERSTAND.
I AM 38 YEARS OLD. I LIVE IN NEW YORK
CITY. I HAVE A FEW KIDS, I AM CHUBBY, WITH
BLACK HAIR.
THANKS
ROSIE

To: STARGAL

From: RO3456

NANCY

IF YOU WATCH THE SHOW TODAY I SAID
HELLO TO NANCY AND KATE AS A WAY OF
INTRODUCING MYSELF, SO WATCH IF YOU
CAN.
LOVE ROSIE

To: RO3456
From: STARGAL
Rosie,
I am so mad at Kate I could kill her, as if we don't
have enough burns already. She doesn't know how
hard it is to make up stories when people ask about
them. When I go to the doctor it is so embarrassing.
We have them all over our chest. It's totally sick.
We're totally sick. I don't know if I can do this much
longer. I can't let this get to me but it always does. I
have to get her next to me and not behind and most
of all never in the front alone. I have to stop her
before she does it but it's so scary. I always think
that if I don't let her burn then she'll shoot our
head off or something stupid like that. She has no
fear, like she is numb to it. Numb to everything she
is stuck on burning and death. That is her ultimate
dream to be dead. She has no consideration for
anyone else. I shouldn't have sent it to you. I
shouldn't have done it. Now I have a crazy 15-year-
old to deal with, I think she's possessed. That is why
she burns.
That's enough babbling I've got to go. Thanks for
listening. Do you ever feel like I do?
Melissa (Nancy)

To: STARGAL
From: RO3456
Hi Mel/Nancy
I forgot to sign off the computer at work last night
so I couldn't sign on from home and no one was at

171

the office to sign me off uggghhhh! I get freaked
out when I have no computer. It's like I'm addicted.
My friends get mad at me and to tell you the truth
so do my kids sometimes because I'd rather write
on this thing than talk . . . hmmmmm.

Well, I'm sorry Kate was so angry about you sending
the letter or her sending it to me. Whoever did it I
appreciate it. I would like to know Kate. What does
she burn you with? And where? Only on your arms?
Maybe we can make a deal when she is really pissed,
she can write me a letter and get it all out. I know
when I am that mad I just want to speak to
someone, to have it heard. Who knows? I will write
her and ask her. I think about you all very often.
And I know, Nancy, it's gonna get better, learning to
trust someone, to be honest and show ALL of who
you are, not just certain pieces. It's what I have to
learn to do too. And hope that people will still love
you afterward. It's a big step.

I am off to do a show, it feels like it never ends,
every day a new show, a kind of fake face . . .
uuuggghh.

Love Rosie

To: RO3456
From: STARGAL
WHY DO I HAVE TO WRITE YOU I DON'T EVEN
KNOW YOU CAN'T TELL ME WHAT I CAN AND
CAN'T DO FUCK YOU IS THAT WHAT YOU
WANT TO HERE FUCK YOU TV CHICK I DON'T
NEED ANYTHING FROM YOU I CAN GET

**WHAT I WANT I CAN GET IT ELSEWHERE I AM
NOT HELPLESS JUST CUZ I GET IT THE ONLY
WAY I NO HOW FUCK ALL OF YOU AND YOU
ARE A FUCKING RELIGIOUS WEIRDO**

To: STARGAL
From: RO3456
I am not a religious weirdo. I am the TV chick, so
what. That doesn't define me. I am someone who
gives a shit, Kate, and you don't scare me and I am
not going to go away.
You are not as tough as you pretend to be. And
neither am I. At some point we all gotta let the
demons out. You are not the only one who has them
and you know what, there ARE people who care, I
am one of them. I don't want anything from you.
I am friends with Stacie, Barb, Nancy, and Melissa. I
like them, a lot. It would suck if it all ended cause
you don't like me, but hell, Kate, you said you are
the boss now so it is up to you. It is easy to be a
roughneck, cursing and telling everyone to die. It is
hard to try to trust that someone can make a
difference. In the eighth grade I had a math teacher
and she helped me see people could make a
difference. Did you ever have anyone, Kate? You
can have me. Are you big enough to do that? And to
leave the body alone? It has had enough hurt
already. . . . You are not alone. You are not the only
one there. Ask everyone else. I haven't fucked up
yet so be brave, gimme a chance. I am not afraid I
am not going away.

The body doesn't deserve any more chaos. So you wanna write me? I would like to know you. Yeah . . .
I know, "fuck you," right?
Well, Kate, that's a cop-out.
Let's see you get real with me, see if you can be big enough to trust.
I love Stacie, I like Nancy, I like Melissa, I don't want you to hurt them anymore, got it?
Try me.
I am not an asshole.
Rosie from TV.

CHAPTER 3 2

It is another Sunday. We are at the same flea market, only the flea market is never the same. Every week, a surprise of sellers, and the regulars: the Huk-A-Poo guy, the tube sock lady, and of course the pickle man.

"Eat a pickle while you're walking. . . ."

That guy could have been a millionaire. He successfully got thousands of people to fork over a quarter and fish out their own two-cent pickle, every Sunday. It was impossible to walk past and not buy one.

"Eat a pickle while you're walking. . . ."

Had he bigger dreams, he could have been Bill Gates. The man had a gift.

I am standing with my mother and sister; I am about to buy a two-eyed dinosaur pocketbook. I had ten dollars, from where, I have no clue. A birthday maybe, a communion, a confirmation, something. I decided to get a handbag. One like my mom had, only not as boring. This was my first real grown-up girl purchase. I wasn't a kid anymore, it was time. I was eight, going on nine.

After much angst, I decided on a mustard-yellow, faux suede shoulder bag. On the front, in appliqué, was a profile of a dinosaur. Had this bag been perfect, it would have cost a bundle, but seeing as this was the flea market, with treasures at every turn, this particular bag was reduced to only eight dollars. Why? Because somewhere in Taiwan or Hong Kong, or wherever faux suede handbags are made, someone got carried away and added an extra eye to the dinosaur, therefore making it "slightly irregular." I liked the bag instantly. We fit together. I, too, felt slightly irregular. Their loss, my gain. I convinced myself you could hardly see the double eye. Unless you were up close, you would miss it, I was sure. No one would notice. I tried the bag on, thinking how I would keep all my secret things inside: whipper-snappers, love letters, and Silly Putty. I needed to make sure no one else had access to it. I had to keep it safe. Yes, I decided, right there, I would have the two-eyed dinosaur faux suede bag with the shoulder strap. I handed the man my ten and got two dollars back. There is no tax at the flea market.

My mother and sister were a few steps in front of me, shopping, stopping, and just looking. I put my grown-up girl handbag on my shoulder and raced toward them, flipping my hair side to

176

side as I ran, just like Marlo Thomas. I looked very grown-up, I thought, with my bag secure on my shoulder.

There are many mysteries to womanhood.

Not all of us are born with the knack for proper pocketbook placement. I, apparently, was not. I looped the strap over my shoulder, without placing my arm in between the straps. I just sort of draped it over my left side, as if I were a kitchen chair. I draped it, and I dashed over to my mother and sister. I didn't say anything about my bag; I waited for them to see it, to comment. They didn't. I kept walking, looking at them, waiting for them to see me and my grown-up dinosaur pocketbook, when a teenage boy came running up behind us, clutching my bag in his hands.

"Lady, your kid dropped this," he said to my mother.

She laughed and thanked the boy/man as I turned four shades of crimson. She put the bag on my shoulder, placed my arm through the strap. She showed me how to lay my hand on the far upper corner, anchoring it. "This way you'll always know it's there." I listened, saying nothing, nodding, embarrassed.

"That's a cute bag, Roseann," she said to me under her breath. "The dinosaur has a double eye." Then she winked.

"Eat a pickle while you're walking."

CHAPTER 33

I am addicted to this computer. Sometimes my hands hurt. Sometimes, after a long spurt of typing, I take two Diet Cokes out of the fridge and roll the cans up and down my arms. It doesn't help much, but it is part of my routine. I love routine.

I am a woman addicted to routine because any shift and God knows what might erupt. I am a woman who will not leave my house alone at night, because there are scary things in the dark. My closest friends can change on me, all in my mind of course. I can stand in front of someone I love, like my sister, Carolyn, or Kelli, and for no reason I understand the planes of their face shift; they transform into strangers before my eyes. I draw in my breath, take a fast step backward. I am difficult to love.

And while my relationship with my multiple was never violent, in its own way it did cause

179

chaos, which I tend to crave. With the exception of Kel and the kids, everyone else came in second to Stacie/Melissa. My friends started to tease me about unreturned phone calls, unanswered mail. . . . "I guess I'm not as exciting as your multiple," one friend said. And, sadly, that friend was right. I checked my e-mail ten times a day. It was more than an urge, it was a compulsion. Did she write me? Which one? Would it be Kate, Nancy, Melissa; would it be Stacie, returned? Tina had told me that Melissa didn't show her alters to anyone—*anyone;* and yet here she was, showing them to me. I felt absurdly flattered. "Superhero RosieO, able to get splintered multiples to appear on command." My multiple was much more exciting than my other friends.

My friends thought I had totally lost it when they heard what was going on. I got a wide range of responses.

"Who do you think you are, Ro?"

"You have no training in this. Back off."

"Has it occurred to you that your correspondence is dangerous? For both of you? You're drawing her out, but where will you be when she needs help tucking it all back in again—have you thought about that, Ro?"

And of course my personal favorite: "Are you out of your ever-loving mind, Roseann?"

Good questions. Smart friends.

* * *

Carolyn, my official skeptic, came over one day. She was not a fan of Stacie's, the phantom fourteen-year-old, and was totally unimpressed with my middle-aged multiple. She thought, like so many people close to me, I should walk away from the whole crazy situation.

"Carolyn," I said. "You don't understand. This woman has been through so much."

"You know what?" said Carolyn. "I don't care what she's been through, Ro, she is no one to me. I think she is taking you for a ride."

"Please, not today," I said. "Look, Carolyn, nothing happens by chance. So let's just leave it, okay?" I stood up and tried to make a dramatic exit.

"Ro," she said, "you've gotta stop talking to her!"

"Why? She's just a woman, and she has a serious psychiatric disorder. That's all."

Carolyn snorted. "MPD is not even a valid psychiatric diagnosis anymore. Insurance companies won't even reimburse for it. It's all part of her hoax."

"Her hoax?" I said. "What kind of hoax?"

"Ro, it is not good. That's what I feel. It is not good."

It's nice to have friends.

I did some of my own research then, and here's what I found about MPD. In fact there *is* some doubt about the validity of the disorder.

Right there in a book I read, "Many doctors think MPD is overdiagnosed, that people use it for money or for forensic reasons or because they need to get attention."

I called a friend of mine who also happens to be a therapist.

"Ro," he said, after I'd gone on for a while, "you want a yes or no. You want it black or white. It isn't that simple."

"Are there documented cases?" I asked him, even though I fully knew there were. It was just reassurance I was looking for.

"Of course there are," he said.

"Have you ever treated one?" I said.

"You," he said.

"Let me do the comedy," I said.

"No, I have never treated one, but that doesn't mean it's not real. . . . I've read case histories."

"Tell me one," I said.

So he did. He told me about the case of a forty-three-year-old woman with twenty-three alters who had different eyeglass prescriptions depending on whose point of view it was on any particular day. He told me about a multiple who responded to Prozac in one alter, imipramine in another. He told me much of what I already knew. Most sufferers are women and have been abused in their childhoods. Many have accompanying intestinal conditions, probably because of stress. Alters can come and go within seconds, or sometimes hours, a slow stretched birth or a sudden snap; boom, the weather changes. Usually some alters are aggressive, like Kate, and others are more passive, like Stacie. Some alters know about the presence of the others; some are completely in the dark. It's one of the weirdest psychiatric conditions. On the one hand, of course, it's hard to believe. Surely no one is capable of that kind of craziness. On the other hand, look around you. Splits are everywhere. Our cells split in cancer, our tongues have a seam in their center, a rift runs right in the middle of our pasty brains, giving us left and right, reason and emotion. When all is said and done, I believe in splits, because so many live in me.

But I did not become a multiple. All the parts of me stayed integrated, connected, aware of each other. A central Rosie was always present, her arms full of music and medicines; whatever was needed. She was the mother in me, I think. The invincible I: on the page, like a pillar. I. I know how to help myself, I always have. This is what makes me different from Melissa: Somewhere in me there's this definite I. My real name, I think, is Ro, which comes from Rose, which is a medicinal flower, used in ancient times for boils and toothaches. Ro. I know something about soothing.

CHAPTER 34

I did not want to go to junior high school. Nobody there knew. Junior high was made up of four different elementary schools, forming one seventh grade. In elementary school everyone knew. I was sure of it. A few months after she died they put up the plaque.

ROSEANN O'DONNELL—WHAT WE ARE GIVEN WE SHALL KEEP.

I walked past it twice a day, on my way to and from the cafeteria. I hated lunch. No one asked me if I wanted a plaque with my and my dead mother's name on it, hung in my school, where everyone would see it every single day, including me. If anyone had asked me, I would have said no.

The only good thing about leaving elementary school was not having to see that plaque. "What we are given we shall keep" was inaccurate. It should have read *What has been taken away we shall pretend never was.*

Seventh grade was scary. Luckily my brother Danny was in ninth grade. He had survived. Maybe I would too. Week one was a disaster.

Mr. Hogan, my English teacher, was collecting homework. I had none. He asked why. I did not answer him. How could I? I didn't have my homework because I never did my homework. My mom was dead, my nana in the hospital, and there was no one home to care if I did my homework or not. So I didn't. I was thirteen, I had other things on my mind.

Mr. Hogan knew none of this, I am sure. How could he? He kept asking for my homework. I kept ignoring him. Finally, exasperated and with nowhere else to go, Mr. Hogan unknowingly dropped the bomb.

"What is your mother's name? I am going to call her and talk to her about you!" The room started to spin. I looked at the floor and blurred my eyes. I heard screaming and sirens as Mr. Hogan's mouth formed the word *mother* over and over, never ending. Then he suddenly stopped. He must have realized something was amiss. I was not a smart-ass. I was troubled.

Kathleen Kennedy was sitting next to me. She did not go to my elementary school, but she knew. From church. She tried to help. She wrote a note on scrap paper, and handed it to me to pass around the class.

"Mr. Hogan is a jerk. He doesn't know Roseann's mom is dead. Now she is sad."

The noise in my head got louder. I got up from my desk and ran out of the classroom, down the stairs, into the street. I ran all the way home.

screaming
running
crashing
crying
wishing, wanting, dreaming
dying

I reached my house. The front door was locked. My normally ever-present nana was in the hospital. I had no way in. I walked across the street to the Nordins', climbed through their basement window, and hid under the pool table, next to the washing machine.

After I went AWOL the school was in a frenzy. Danny was called down to the principal's office and questioned. Where would I go? they wanted to know. He didn't have a clue. They took Danny in a police car and drove him around the neighborhood calling to me over the loudspeaker.

"Roseann, it's Danny . . . where are you . . . you are not in trouble . . . Mr. Hogan is a jerk. . . ."

I stayed under the pool table and thought about hurting myself. The phone rang and rang and rang; finally I picked it up. It was my dad, he was at work. He told me I was not in trouble.

That I should go outside and tell everyone I was okay. I told my dad he had to come get me, and he did.

That night I decided I was never going back to school again in my whole entire life. A week later my father brought me back to school to meet with the assistant principal. She was a short round woman who thought she could help. She could not. I sat in her office, staring at my sneakers, silently counting backward from a thousand as she waxed poetic about grief, sorrow, and being different. I would not speak to her. After an hour, she gave up.

Two days later I went back to school unaware of my good fortune. Things had changed. All the teachers were extra nice to me. Mr. Hogan gave me an undeserved A. Most importantly, now in junior high, everyone knew.

CHAPTER 35

I hated chemistry, back in high school. The periodic table, the one that supposedly showed how the world was made, made no sense to me. At all. It was Egyptian hieroglyphics, pig Latin, Morse code, it was pure gibberish. I learned only one thing the entire year: Some chemicals and minerals are inherently unstable; others, even in liquid form, have a certain solidity, so no matter how high you heat them or deep you freeze them they retain their essential structure. Ether evaporates as soon as it hits the air. But diamonds, you can't destroy a diamond. You can't destroy iridium, osmium, mercury, which have the highest melting point of all metals. Tungsten was my favorite, for the way it popped on the tongue, and for its strength. It was a beautiful orange crystal that fluoresced bright blue in ultraviolet light.

Why, I want to know, are some substances inherently unstable while others can hold up even under mammoth pressures? I suppose no one knows the answer to this; why grace hits here and not there, why strengths emerge or don't.

I have the same question about people. Why can two people with certain similarities in their histories, from similar economic backgrounds, offered similar opportunities, wind up in such different places? Why does one person turn tungsten, another ether? Why did Melissa split? Why did I not? Melissa lived in a trailer with a leaky roof and no shower. I live in a brownstone with maple floors and pocket doors. Melissa, despite her alters, has so few people. I have, in a solidly real sense, so many.

I once read that a few good memories can be the means of saving us. I don't know who wrote that, but the line has stayed in my mind. I began to think: What are my memories—not the bad ones, but the ones that have helped me get through?

I remember my mother baking during a snowstorm; calling us all to the table, serving us still-warm cookies with a glass of cold milk. I remember teaching my baby brother Timmy to play chess, and him beating me six months later. I remember loving my sister, always. I remember Eddie taking me to see *A Chorus Line*. Danny trying to find me when I ran away from school. I remember the Ellards' house, with dust ruffles and good-morning kisses. I remember learning to drive. Driving alone in the car with the windows rolled up, saying out loud the secret thoughts I had only before whispered inside my head. I remember teaching myself to juggle, to balance a chair on one finger, to spin a basketball. I remember Barbra Streisand, newborn babies, teachers who favored me. I remember sticking up for the underdogs and feeling, at those moments, certain of my strength, of my goodness, a kind of centering in me. I remember getting up extra early so I could get the toy surprise out of the Froot Loops. I remember learning to read . . . D-O-G and how the dashes went away and sustenance appeared. Chapter books and library trips, and magical worlds waiting to be fallen into. I remember Ring Dings cakes, how you bit into the darkness and an ooze of white cream appeared—*there*. I remember Bette Midler singing from a place few can. I remember, from some of my earliest moments, what I can only call a *will to live;* perhaps this is the difference, a kind of chemical urge that some are blessed with, others not.

Is it, therefore, luck that I became in some senses a winner? Rich, successful, funny, and famous. Endless opportunity at every turn. I won, I think, the chemical lottery. I was blessed with enough whatever it was to get to wherever it is I am.

How can I ever really know the answer to this? I think it does have something to do with an innate faith that no one could sway me from. A sense that the world had meaning, and part of that meaning was me. I was *meant* for something. Life is so full of twists, split seconds where you could go left or right, and that small decision determines all that comes after it. Perhaps if I had *not* gone to B.U., and had *not* had a professor who told me I had no talent and whom I had to rebel against, and I find, now at almost forty, I am still rebelling against, perhaps I would not have become a stand-up comic. Perhaps if we had lived just one neighborhood over, and the Ellards were not my neighbors, and there was no Jackie or Buster Brown shoes to teach me about longing. Perhaps perhaps. Perhaps if on the night my parents made me it had been rainy, and a Y joined up with an X . . . a million coincidences combined to make me me, and Melissa, Melissa. We are passive participants, this is what I think.

The most fragile line of chance separates a woman like me from a woman like Melissa. So many similarities, but so many essential differences. *If this,* or *if that,* and I could be her. I could have no central I, no essential pillar of self. I saw myself, my splits, in Melissa, for sure. I also saw deep, deep differences. Mostly what I saw was grace, in that "there but for the grace of God go I."

CHAPTER 36

Sometime around Christmas, six months after my summer with Stacie had started, I agreed to take a role in the Broadway musical *Seussical*. I danced and sang and wore the Cat's red hat while the Sour Kangaroo sold it to the back row every night, leaving the audience screaming for more. I love Broadway. I love the lights like giant pearls around the placards, and sweaty dressing rooms. On Broadway, show business is almost as good as I dreamed it could be.

During rehearsals I realized it was time to meet Melissa. I began to fantasize about it. What would she look like? Act like? Would she split into another in front of me? Would I be able to tell it was happening? I was excited at the thought, overwhelmingly curious. It would be an adventure, a thrill; frankly, I couldn't wait. I decided to invite Tina too, as I didn't want Melissa to be alone in New York City. I wanted her to feel safe, for the trip to be a positive one. I wondered if she would come.

I told some friends this brilliant idea, flying in my multiple, meeting her in person. They all thought I was nuts. Some thought I was kidding.

"You can't be serious!"

I was dead serious.

"Aren't you scared?"

Of course I wasn't scared.

"What if she is dangerous?"

She wasn't dangerous.

I was sure of it, I knew her, this stranger I had never seen. I "met" Melissa/Stacie in May, and this was February we were talking about, a good nine months. We were friends. I was shocked so many people freaked out at the concept. I did not understand their concerns. At all.

I e-mailed Melissa and asked if she would be interested. She said she didn't know. She had never been on a plane before, never been to New York City. "No, it's too weird. . . . I don't think it is a good idea." I was surprised; I expected her to want to come. She didn't. After a lot of pushing, she told me why. She was afraid that after I met her, I would no longer be interested in being her friend. I gasped aloud when I read that on the e-mail. I got a little misty-eyed. She was worried I would reject her. I knew I never would.

She finally agreed to come. I used my appearing on Broadway as a leverage point. It would be fun, and chances were, it would be my last Broadway show for a long, long time. For me, the setting had something to do with my wanting her there. The fact that night after night I was on stage, surrounded by people playing all these different parts. There is something magical about Broadway, the crowds, the velvet plush seats, the pinging of a violin tuning up before the swell of the orchestra hits you with full force. I love it, so much. My mother loved it too. I wanted Melissa to get to experience it. Secretly I hoped Stacie might show up for a few minutes, to catch just a glimpse of the dancing, the color-ful costumes of choreographed masses moving in time. I wanted to give her Broadway, like my mom had given it to me.

I sent the tickets. I started the countdown, like a kid waiting for Christmas. One month to Melissa, three weeks, and then just twenty-four hours.

On the day before she arrived, I dreamed of her. She was lost in the streets of Manhattan. I was out driving around in a double-decker bus, looking for her. I would catch her in the crowd, this woman I had never met, never seen a photo of; I would find her. And when I called out her name, she would vanish.

The plan was this. She and Tina would fly in Thursday night. Jimmy, my hippie surfer-dude driver, would pick them up and take them to their hotel. Then, Friday morning, they would come see the TV show. We would hang out for lunch, then I would finish my workday and meet them for dinner at Joe Allen's, my favorite restaurant on Forty-sixth Street. After that we would head over to the Richard Rodgers Theatre. They'd watch me do my *Cat in the Hat* gig and then meet me in my dressing room, post-show. We'd hang out a little. I had a Saturday matinee and was wiped from a week of double duty, TV and theater, so it would have to be an early night for me. They could spend the rest of their evening doing whatever they wanted. I assumed they would go back to the hotel and sleep. Saturday, I would get them tickets for a matinee, then meet them in between shows for dinner; they would go see another show Saturday night. Sunday morning, they would all go home. I had scheduled each and every moment. Control issues? Who is to say?

I felt like cruise director Julie McCoy. "Right this way, your cabin is on the promenade deck. You'll enjoy a complimentary cheese platter in your room. Shuffleboard at noon."

Carolyn said, "I bet you a million bucks they don't show."

"Why would they not show?" I said.

"Because, don't you see," she said, "it's to their benefit to remain mysterious. The mystery keeps you hooked, and they know that, Ro. They know, sooner or later, you're gonna send them money, as long as you remain hooked."

"They'll show," I said.

*　　*　　*

And they did.

D-Day. Due date. I was more excited than nervous. I had Jimmy call me after he dropped them safely at the hotel. I pumped him for details. Being Jimmy, he just said, "They were cool. . . . Man . . . it is all good." Life, for Jimmy, is "all good, man."

I got up early that morning, the day I was to meet her. I was in the office by 7 A.M. tingling with excitement. I kept asking my assistant if they had arrived yet . . . no, no, no. It was almost nine o'clock, time for me to get into makeup. I was walking down the hall with my comedy producer, friend, and fellow swamp person Janette. Janette was the only person who knew about my relationship with Melissa and understood it, who found it as fascinating as I did. She thought it was perfectly logical we should meet, me and Melissa. "What a great idea!"—that's what she said when I told her. "Of course you two should meet!" That's why I love Janette, she makes me feel less alone.

I was nervous. I was meeting her, but in my mind it was more than that. Brace yourself. I felt I was meeting me, what I might have been, had grace gone down a little differently, had chance dealt out a different hand.

So Janette and I are walking the same route we have every morning for the last five years. We turn the corner, as always, and head toward the dressing room, and I stop. I think I should go check and see if she is in the green room, on the off chance they got upstairs without Merrie knowing. It is a long shot, but it is just down the hall. I turn around; Janette follows me, without missing a beat. I see an attractive sixty-something woman standing by the bathroom, looking at my disheveled self, trying to see if it is, in fact, me. It is. "Rosie," she says, smiling. It's Tina, Melissa's shrink; I recognize her voice from the phone. We say our hellos and she walks me toward the green room, where Melissa is waiting. "Is she okay?" I ask.

"So far, yes. She is nervous to meet you." That calms me a little. I'm not the only one nervous.

She is standing with her back to me. Tina calls her name gently, and I wait for her eyes to meet mine. They do, for only a moment, she then looks away quickly. I give her a hug and make small talk as I notice the burns on her hands, the fear in her face. I am almost in performance mode, a switch I make at least twenty times a day. In and out of "Rosie" back to Ro. I entertain Melissa, trying to put her at ease. It is for her, after all, this switch I do, so she will feel okay. That's what I tell myself, but I know it is also for me. It is my armor, my deflector shield, my fame suit. It protects me from humanity, from vulnerability, from being real.

She is my age, and bigger than I am. She has dark hair and wears glasses. She does not feel like a stranger. I sat there and looked at Melissa, who embodied Stacie and Barb and Doug. I looked at this woman, separated from me by only the thinnest, most breakable line. I caught myself staring. Melissa looked uncomfortable. She toed the floor. She said, "Thanks for all this, Rosie. I can't believe it is really happening." Then she gave a very sweet smile, a smile I can surely say was genuine.

I went into makeup and got ready for the show. I was sort of numb, trying to stay in my body and feel everything as it was happening. At times of great emotion, good or bad, I find I am gone, somewhere else, watching it happen to me, a different me. I miss a lot of my own life, my own moments, because I step outside myself. I feel it all more in retrospect than in actual time. My iMovies make me cry, but while filming the event that caused such emotion, I feel nothing. I am always once removed, sometimes twice.

I walked through the curtain to music and applause. I spotted them right away. They were six rows up, on the left-hand side, on the aisle. I was completely distracted the whole show. I do not remember the guests that day, but I do remember that Melissa laughed seven times, blew her nose once, and took off her glasses during the commercials to rub her eyes, as if she had a headache. I hoped she didn't have a headache. I worried that headaches were precursors to switching. Sally Field in *Sybil*, she always got a

headache, and then "the people . . . the people."
Was she switching? I didn't think so. Tina was by
her side, absorbed in the show, enjoying herself.
Tina was not troubled; this I took as a good sign.
I always go to the faces of those in the know, to
check, to see, to take the temperature. I like to
know when I am in trouble. During turbulence
on a flight, I search for the stewardess. If she is
buckled in and pale, then I worry. If not, I con-
tinue on as usual, no matter how bumpy it becomes.

The show ended. They came back to my of-
fice, and we ordered in sandwiches and chatted.
"So," I said, "how was the plane ride?"
"Good," Melissa said. "I've never stayed in a
hotel before."
"Never, ever?" I said, disbelieving.
"Not once."

We talked about room service. They both were
amazed to find a glass of orange juice cost sixteen dollars; a bagel, twelve. Tina said she had
something for the both of us, Melissa and I. She
opened her bag and took out two identical In-
dian change purses, with beads on the front and
zippers on the top. She handed each of us one.
As I went to take it from her, she held on to my
hand, and then did the same with Melissa. The
three of us were sitting, connected by a triangle
of arms, in total quiet. Tina looked at both of us,

her eyes tearing up. "I don't know how this happened, that you two found a way to help each other, two strangers. I am so touched by both of you, your courage, your caring. I wanted to give you this as a token of this weekend, the power of faith, in learning to trust." It was at once awkward and then not. Melissa looked down, and at Tina, not at me. She thanked Tina, and opened the purse, as did I. Inside was a small gray stone with a Chinese symbol on it, and a piece of paper, explaining it. Mine said, "Courage—not the absence of fear or despair, but the strength to conquer them." I am not sure what Melissa's said; I didn't have the courage to ask.

I met them for dinner, at six o'clock. My body, by this time, felt almost limpid, like I had gotten to the other side of a great fright and had just reached the coming-down, the slowing-up. Here she was—my multiple, my Melissa, and the really strange thing was her ordinariness. She was plain. She blew her nose. She had shy eyes and aching bones and over lunch she tapped two Tylenols into her palm. Yes, she had burns; yes, there was evidence of great distress, but seeing it up close, even the burns became oddly not odd, just something she did to get by, just one more quirk of human nature.

The dinner, too, was calm, peaceful, not at all what I expected. There was no drama, at all. We talked about movies and children and Target. In the very end, which was also sort of a beginning, we were just three women, sitting like so many other women in so many other restaurants, chatting about life, three spoons and a single slice of chocolate cake.

We made our way to the theater. They saw my tiny dressing room, complete with my Power-Book, on which most nights I would write Melissa during intermission. My assistant Bobby got them to their seats and came back for all the dirt. *"Tell me!"* he said in that Bobby way. I smiled. There wasn't a lot to tell. She was nice, normal, ordinary. She was Melissa, not "my multiple" anymore.

The Melissa I'd met, however, was not the Melissa of my mind. It was the fantasy Melissa, and the fantasy Melissa's fantasy of Stacie, that I had fallen for, a long hall of mirrors that ended, finally, with a reflection of myself. That night, after the show, after I'd said good-bye to them and arrived back at my house, I felt somewhat sad. I felt something was over, a kind of intensity, a misplaced curiosity. What would bind me to her, now that I knew? There was no Stacie. Now I had nothing left between me and me.

There was a lemon wafer of a moon out, and the fence made its familiar filigree pattern on the courtyard as I looked down from the window. Good-bye girl.

CHAPTER 37

Mrs. Nordin took us to the flea market every Sunday after my mother died. The five of us, the three of them, and her, all piled in their new white station wagon.

But the flea market wasn't the same. It was the absence of her that was with me that Sunday, my first time back after her death. Her lack of presence, her nothingness. Her being, just gone.

I wanted dungarees. Blue jeans, cool and tough and exactly what I needed. I knew they were expensive, sixteen dollars. I went to the booth alone, clutching my twenty in my pocket. I could do this by myself. I didn't need anyone. Not a mother, not a neighbor posing as one.

The dungaree man was very popular. His booth was crowded, three or four people deep. As I waited my turn I read the cardboard sign on the top of his open-ended station wagon. In runny red Magic Marker it said JEANS—$16—ALL SALES FINAL.

I made my way to the front of the table. Major action: Money was passed back and forth, jeans were flying left and right. The man taking the cash was harried and sweaty. There are no try-on booths in the flea market. People know their size, they walk up and scream it out confidently—"Twenty-eight/thirty-two"—what they want appears in front of them ten seconds later. You have to be quick at the flea market.

"What do you need?" the man asked while wiping his forehead with a damp cloth. "What size?"

Oh no. My heart started to pound. I saw the masking tape, with the sizes written in code: twenty-eight/thirty . . . thirty-two/thirty-eight . . . thirty-thirty. It was my turn. I was eleven. I had never bought myself anything. My now-dead mother bought all my clothes. I did not know my size. I stood, staring, clutching my twenty, looking lost, confused, taking way too much time. Then the sweaty man, frustrated at my silence, said, "Where is your mother, kid? Who is with this little one? Where's your mother?"

Everything stopped. I felt my blood pumping in my skull, a dull thud, a broken stereo, the bass way up. In the movie version, everything would fade to black-and-white slow motion. A tight shot of the jean man's face, mouthing *mother* over and over. Quick cut to my eleven-year-old eyes, then the jeans, then a ball of sweat dripping down the man's neck, then the masking-tape numbers, then me, again, out of focus, with a handheld camera, all jiggly, like *NYPD Blue*. A siren would start, low, off in the distance, the cuts would get quicker, the siren louder, until finally it would land on me, as I screamed "thirty/thirty" as loud as I could, shoving my money toward the camera lens.

That's what I did. I took a thirty/thirty, knowing all sales were final. I gave away sixteen dollars, willingly, anything to make it stop. I did not want to hear that question again. I did not want anyone to answer it. I got my four dollars change and my way-too-big jeans in a plastic bag.

On the long drive home, I had the way, way back all to myself. Using my jeans as a pillow, I watched the treetops pass. We turned the corner and made our way up the steep hill of Harned Road with no trouble, no trouble at all.

I squeezed my eyes tight, and listened for her voice. Some tears spilled out as I tried to conjure it, without success. It had already faded from my memory.

CHAPTER 38

So she left. She got on a plane Sunday morning and went back to Ashland, taking my obsession with her in a carry-on.

Life came back into focus, perspective shifted back to somewhere near normal. I did not think about her twenty-four/seven, like I used to. In fact it was nearly a week before I checked my e-mails. When I did, this was waiting for me.

To: RO3456
From: STARGAL
Hi Rosie, this is Stacie, I saw you on there on the stage for a minute. No one would let me come up front, but I saw you, and the music, from my velvet seat. I got scared and then someone else came. I also saw you in the restaurant, when we all shared a dessert. I like dessert the most of everyone. No one lets me come up much now. I think maybe you are mad but we know you aren't but I think it is all so

crazy. Then Nancy tells me it is okay and I didn't do nothing. Thanks for helping me with the baby. I don't know what happened to it, I think it is dead, but that's okay cause nobody did it. Did you know that Justin may leave 'NSYNC and join the Backstreet Boys? The Backstreet Boys have no smell. They smell average.
Stacie

And that was it, the last I heard from Stacie. It would be a better ending if it turned out Melissa was an ex-con and had swindled millions out of unsuspecting idiots like me. Or if she ended up being my sister, or a man. There are so many endings that would work. The realizations I came to, through this relationship, were at once subtle and profound:

Saving the world is a lofty goal and an impossible feat.
Swimming in others' pain only delays the journey through your own.
I have many parts but only one self.
Fame fixed none of the things I wanted it to.
It is time for me to leave my show.

We are friends, Melissa and I. We communicate mostly by e-mail, although we have each other's numbers in case of emergency. She seems shocked when I call her just to chat, and I have, since that night on Broadway. I touch base, seeing if she is okay, checking, I think, that I am too. I like her, my friend Melissa. She has given me many things, parts of myself I had locked away.

Nothing happens by chance.

CHAPTER 39

I am not sure if I believe that dead people stay with us after they go—their souls lingering as we, the left, live out our earth lives. Some people do. John Edwards, Sylvia Brown, they have made a career and millions of dollars off this concept. I want to believe it. I just can't seem to.

I went for a reading, a chat, a conversation, two different times, with two different mediums. Both were amazingly inaccurate. My mother was there, they each assured me, saying cryptic things. It doesn't make sense to me. If a spirit is going to take the time and energy required—and one would assume that to be a lot—to make itself heard, why would it speak in riddles? "She said you know someone whose name starts with a T."

My mother was many things, but never vague. She would have said something witty and wise, something clever and conclusive. Something like "eat a pickle while you're walking" or "under the Ming vase" or just "Limoges."

"Someone with a T" is so not her.

• • •

Parker got a LEGO soccer game for Christmas. He ripped the red and green wrapping paper, saw the corner, and screamed, "He did it, Mama! Santa got my letter! He did it!"

LEGO soccer, thirty-seven dollars.

His face on Christmas morning . . . priceless.

I assembled the LEGO soccer stadium (no easy task), and the games began. He can beat me for real, which I find shocking, as I have thirty-three years on the kid. He is quite good. The score was tied at two all; next goal was winner, we both agreed. We were taunting each other in the Little League way:

"Prepare to lose, Fred."

"Keep dreaming, Mama."

"You're dead meat, squirt."

"And you are fart mashed potatoes."

"Don't say fart, turd man."

"Okay, turd mom."

There was a lull in our verbal Ping-Pong as he lined up a shot from the backfield. He let the ball go, and as he did, he said, "Come on, Bessie!" clear as day.

I sat there stunned. Had I misheard? "What did you say, Park?" I asked him.

"Come on, Bessie," he said again.

Huge multiple spingle.

I asked him why he said that. "I don't know, Mama, it just came in my head."

He won that game with his "Come on, Bessie" shot. He sailed the ball right past me as I watched him with watery eyes. He left the room with a wink.

Come on, Bessie. Hello, Mom.